GREEK ISLANDS
OF THE AEGEAN
—*in your pocket*—

PHOTOGRAPH CREDITS

Travel Library/James Davis Travel Photography 5,
10, 13, 14, 15, 16, 17, 18, 21, 22, 23, 24, 29, 35, 36,
37, 39, 40, 41, 42, 45 (top), 48, 55, 56, 59, 60, 63,
66, 67, 74, 75 (top, bottom), 78 (top, bottom), 79,
84, 89, 95, 96, 97 (top, bottom), 98, 100, 106, 108,
111, 113, 117 (top, bottom), 119, 121, 125; Travel
Library 8, 12, 31, 51, 52, 72, 73, 76, 77, 87, 102,
105; Travel Library/Philip Enticknap 85, 122;
Travel Library/R Richardson front cover, back
cover, title page, 7, 11, 47, 64, 69, 70, 80, 83, 91, 92,
114; Travel Library/G Walden 45 (bottom); CM
Dixon 26.

*Front cover: Blue and white church, Santorini; back
cover: beach with boat, Mykonos; title page: donkey with
vegetable baskets*

MANUFACTURE FRANÇAISE DES PNEUMATIQUES MICHELIN

Société en commandite par actions au capital de 2 000 000 000 de francs

Place des Carmes-Déchaux – 63 Clermont-Ferrand (France)

R.C.S. Clermont-Fd 855 200 507

© Michelin et Cie. Propriétaires-Éditeurs 1996

Dêpôt légal Avril 96 – ISBN 2-06-650301-0 – ISSN en cours

Printed in the EU 3-96

CONTENTS

INTRODUCTION

Over 3 000 islands form the Aegean
archipelago, from small rocks protruding
from reefs to large islands like Chios and
Lesbos. Each of the inhabited islands,
irrespective of its size, is unique in its setting
and character. Each island also is part of
history, part of the Greek civilization which
was born upon it, and which influences the
Western world's way of life to this day.

The 'Wine-dark Sea'

During the Mesozoic period, a great land
mass covered the area from Constantinople
to Crete. This land mass later sank during
the Tertiary period leaving only the tips of
the mountain ranges above the sea, which
are today's archipelago. It was during this
geological upheaval that the waters of the
Atlantic Ocean entered the Mediterranean
basin through the straits of Gibraltar – the
pillars of Hercules – to form the
Mediterranean Sea. The Aegean, Homer's
'wine-dark sea', was born.

The name 'Aegean' has been explained
in different ways. The legendary explanation
is the one which Greek schoolchildren
learn. When Theseus – son of the King of
Athens – returned from Crete after slaying
the Minotaur, he forgot to change the sails
of his ship from black to white, as he had
agreed with his father to do, to show that he
was alive and well. Aegeus, standing on top
of the cliffs at Cape Sounion, saw the black
sails and thought that Theseus was dead,
killed by the Minotaur. In his grief he threw
himself from the cliff. The sea in which
Aegeus died so tragically was named after
him so that we would always remember the
father of Theseus.

The other explanation is rather more prosaic. Most coastal towns in Ancient Greece were called Aegae. Names beginning with the stem 'Aeg' denote water: the sea, springs or rivers. (Zeus was also called 'Aegiohos' to indicate his power to command storms.) It follows that coastal towns dependent upon the sea could, in time, give their name to the sea.

Rugged coastlines, like this on Skíathos, can be found on most of the Greek islands.

HOW TO USE THIS GUIDE

This guide is divided into four main
sections:

Background sets the scene, with an
introduction to how the Greek Islands were
formed; an outline of their rich history and
culture, including the legends and heroes;
and information on how to plan your trip,
including when, where and how to go.
The **Island Descriptions** form the main part
of the book and look at each of the island
groups in turn: the Cyclades, the
Dodecanese, the Sporades, islands of the
eastern and northern Aegean, and islands of
the Saronic Gulf. Within each island group,
the main islands and many of the smaller
islands that are accessible to tourists are
treated in alphabetical order. At the end of
each island description, there is a summary
section that includes some basic information
including the island's size and population,
how to reach the island and what
connections are available to other islands for
those who want to go island-hopping.
Enjoying Your Visit provides friendly, no-
nonsense advice on day-to-day holiday
activities that can make the difference
between a good holiday and a great one,
namely swimming and watersports, and what
and where to eat and drink.
A-Z Factfinder is an easy-to-use reference
section packed with useful information,
covering everything you may need to know
on your visit, from tipping to hiring cars,
from using the telephone to vaccinations. A
word of warning: opening hours and
telephone numbers frequently change, so be
sure to check with a local tourist office when
planning your visit.

*Mykonos, the most
cosmopolitan island
in the Aegean, and
one of the busiest,
yet still a beautiful
place to visit.*

HISTORY

The island-studded Aegean, with its brilliantly translucent waters, may have been where man first learned to master the sea around 10 000 years ago. The proximity of the islands to each other made them natural stepping stones to a new seafaring civilization.

The early Cycladic culture and the peaceful Minoan civilization are dealt with in the introduction to the Cyclades. By around 1500 BC the warlike Mycenaeans dominated the Aegean from their massively walled mainland cities. Their culture was swept away in 1150 BC by the aggressive Dorians invading from the North. At this time, Phoenician merchants from the Levant controlled trade in the Aegean, and with trade came civilizing ideas from older cultures. Out of this melting pot came the

The secluded island of Alónissos in the Sporades.

8

genius of Greek civilization which was already unique and vital by the 8C BC.

It is the geographical position of the Aegean which has made it so important historically, lying as it does between the civilizations of the East and West. The pivotal moment in Greek history came in the 5C BC. Greece could easily have become part of the vast Persian Empire: with Greece under Eastern influence, European history would have been different. But Greece – a small country fighting the resources of an entire empire, its forces hopelessly outnumbered – would not be conquered. In a series of battles which truly were heroic, Persia was turned back.

This marked the beginning of Greece's Golden Age. Athens became the leading sea power in the Mediterranean, and the Aegean islands were quickly retaken. Over the following centuries Greek colonies were established as far away as Spain, France and North Africa, as well as Sicily and the Black Sea. During the Peloponnesian War (431-404 BC) most of the islands supported Athens, some – like Milos – Sparta. Important islands such as Lesbos and Chios changed sides when it suited them. But whatever their politics, all were Greek.

By the 2C BC, Greece was being gradually eclipsed by Rome. Briefly, at the beginning of the 1C BC, Mithradates threatened Rome from the East and seized most of the Aegean except Rhodes. But by the Battle of Actium in 31 BC all of Greece and its islands had become part of the Roman Empire. The island of Delos thrived as a trading centre, but generally the Aegean waned in importance.

With the collapse of Rome and its empire in the West, the seat of power moved East

again to Byzantium (modern Istanbul),
modestly renamed Constantinople in 330 AD
by the Emperor Constantine. Christianity,
which already flourished in several parts of
Greece, now became the official religion of
the Roman Empire. Once more, the Aegean
became important.

For centuries the Byzantine fleet with its
Dromones dominated the eastern
Mediterranean. But every empire has its day.
By the time the Venetians sacked Constan-
tinople in 1204, the Aegean islands had

*Remains of a statue
of Apollo lying
beside a hilltop
road in Náxos.*

10

An example of Byzantine work. This fresco can be seen at St John's Monastery in Patmos.

known centuries of murder and pillage by Saracen pirates.

The rise of Venetian sea power changed the fortunes of the islands yet again. Their fortifications were reinforced to protect them from marauding Moor and Saracen pirates and to provide safe harbour and safe passage for the Venetian mercantile fleet. Venice's 'Lion of St Mark' can still be seen on many fortifications today. Venice held sway in the Aegean until the 16C, although Genoa also controlled some islands, including Chios, Lesbos and, later, Rhodes. This left a significant Catholic minority on the islands, especially in the Cyclades.

From the 14C a new power had been rising in the East – the Turks. In 1453 they had taken Constantinople, and the islands fell to them one by one. Ottoman rule put the

A Venetian watch tower in Alónissos.

whole Aegean in a state of limbo: it became a backwater. However, Greek shipping was gaining importance all the time as the Turks – a non-seafaring race – slowly entrusted their shipping to the Greeks. By the 18C, Greek-owned and Greek-crewed merchant ships were criss-crossing the Aegean and Mediterranean. These ships were to form the Greek navy when the Greek War of Independence began in 1821. All of the islands helped free Greece from Turkish rule, but most significantly, Spetses, Hydra and Psara. With Independence, in 1832, the Cyclades and one or two other islands came under Greek rule. Only after the end of the Balkan Wars in 1913 were all the islands, with the exception of Imbros and Tenedos, returned to Greece.

A view of Hydra's harbour, which had a significant role in the Greek War of Independence.

During the 20C, Greece has suffered many tragedies: defeat and genocide in the Anatolian Campaign (1922); Italian, German and Bulgarian invasions during World War II, followed by widespread starvation; Civil War (1947-1949); and a Colonel's junta (1967-1974). But the Greeks are a clear-headed and resourceful nation. This people, which produced Aristotle and Sappho, Odysseus and Zorba will no doubt approach the 21C with the same genius and lust for life it has shown in the last 30C or so.

PLANNING YOUR TRIP

The Traveller

If you are the kind of person who likes order, punctuality and a predictable holiday, perhaps you should consider a Rhine cruise rather than island hopping in the Aegean. Greek ferries do not always leave or arrive when they are supposed to; when the weather is bad (Aegean squalls are notorious) they are often cancelled or change route.

The inter-island ferry Sifnos Express *in dock at Náxos.*

Plumbing is approximate on the islands. Waiters tend to serve you when they feel like it, especially in the high season. You will always find somewhere to stay (especially if you are first off the ferry) but it may take perseverance on the more remote islands in busy periods. But if you can adapt to the relaxed, easy-going life of the islands – using this guide to avoid some frustrations and taking the ones you cannot avoid in your stride – you will have the holiday of a lifetime. Nothing can prepare you for the brilliant light, the pellucid water, the history all around you and the warmth of the people.

Evening light casts shadows in the fishing harbour at Naousa in Páros.

When to Go
The best months are either May and June or September, and even October, which can be unsettled, but you may be lucky with the 'little summer of St Dimitrios'. The peak months, July and August, are very hot, the ferries, beaches and accommodation crowded, and the Meltémi wind at its most boisterous.

Where to Go
Do not set off with the idea that you are going to see a great many islands – unless you can devote several months to it. And even then you will have rather missed the

point. Make friends with a handful of islands, and next time a handful more. The Greek islands are like people: those which become your favourites you may not like immediately. It all takes time.

Once you have arrived, leave an island when the spirit moves you. Or stay put if you like it enough – become a Lotus Eater. But it is necessary to plan in advance which islands, in which group, you think you might like to visit. The Aegean is much larger than you suppose: taking a ferry is an interesting experience but it is a mistake to spend a disproportionate amount of time doing it.

The Greeks are a warm and friendly people.

We have given thumbnail sketches of a wide selection of islands, trying to capture the unique spirit of each place by describing the history, topography and traditions which give each island a special character. Alongside this are details of beaches and other important holiday considerations.

First-time travellers should seriously consider planning their trip around a group of islands in the Cyclades, where there is great variety, or possibly the more distant Dodecanese, close to Turkey. Another option is to start more gently by taking a direct flight to a larger, more developed island – perhaps on a package holiday – visiting nearby islands if and when you feel like it.

How to Go

If you prefer the sound of an island-hopping holiday, choose a base island which you like, and which has good connections to other islands that interest you. To save precious time at the beginning, there may be a direct flight to your chosen base, or a Greek internal flight (*see* information section under each island) from Athens. Of course, the cheapest way is an economy fare to Athens and ferries all the way! Then, if you have the time and the inclination, you can wander across the sea like Odysseus…

A great way to see the islands is by boat, such as this tourist boat moored off Ía, Santoríni.

THE CYCLADES

The sacred island of Delos was the spiritual
and commercial hub of the Classical World.
The islands which surround it became
known as the Cyclades, from *kyklos,* the
Greek for circle. But 2 000 years before that
another civilization flourished here. Known
as the Cycladic culture, it reached its zenith
between 2700-2300 BC.

*The blue-domed
church looks out
from Santoríni over
the vast Aegean
Sea.*

Archaeological finds show that the
islanders were skilled seafarers and traders.
The small idols they made, mainly from
marble quarried in Páros, are among the

world's great art treasures. The idols depict mainly women, probably goddesses, in an abstract, geometric way that is strangely modern. This haunting sculpture can be seen in the National Archaeological Museum and at the Goulandris Museum of Cycladic Art, both in Athens, and in the Archaeological Museum of Náxos.

The islands were ruled by Crete from 2000 to c.1500 BC. The cataclysmic explosion of the volcano on Santoríni, which gave rise to the legend of Atlantis, brought an end to the peaceful Minoan (Cretan) civilization. The islands were then colonized by the Ionians, displaced by the movement of the Dorians south along the Greek peninsula (*see* **History** p.8). With the flowering of Greek civilization, the Cyclades — with Delos at their heart – became the political and religious centre of the Aegean archipelago. Control of the Cyclades was a political weather vane, since the islands allied themselves to the most powerful state of the time as circumstances changed. The islands were ruled in turn from Athens, Sparta, Macedonia, but during the Roman Empire their importance declined and some of them were used as places of exile. (Indeed, some islands have been put to the same use as recently as 1967-1974 during the Colonels' dictatorship).

During the Byzantine Empire, the decline of the islands continued, with the possible exception of Andros. They were constantly sacked by pirates, mainly Saracens. After the fall of Constantinople, control of the Cyclades became important to the great trading empire of Venice and their ruined castles and fortifications can be seen on most islands. The islands were finally overrun by the Turks in the 1580s. The islanders took part in the Greek Revolution of 1821, and following the 1830 Treaty of London became part of Greece. During World War II, while in Axis hands, the Cyclades were quite heavily bombed: the target of both Greek and British commando raids.

AMORGÓS

dramatic cliffs – magnificent views – a sacred icon – a magic oracle

Amorgós is a long, narrow, rugged island, that appears like a hog's back rising from the sea. Climb up to Minoa, above Katápola, for spectacular **views** from the ruined temple of Apollo. Hóra (meaning 'place' and used on many of the islands as the name for the capital) has a Venetian castle (and the smallest church in Greece), but the greatest attraction is the **Hozoviótissa Monastery**. Built by monks from Palestine in the 9C, destroyed by pirates, and rebuilt in 1088, it houses an icon of the Virgin Mary which is said to have arrived unaccompanied at night in a shining boat. Also miraculous is the **Laloussa spring** at another monastery, that of Agios Giorgios Balsamitís. It is said you can see the future when you look into the water.

Information: The south-facing beaches are better, especially the deserted ones towards the southern tip of the island, if you have your own transport.

Port: Katápola

Size: 124km^2 (48sq miles)

Population: 1 800

How to get there: By ferry from Piraeus; also from Rafína

Connections: Caique to Náxos in season.

ANÁPHI (ANÁFI)

tamarisk-fringed sand – walking – caves – windmills – a mountainous interior

The god Apollo made this island rise from the sea to give refuge to the Argonauts during a terrible storm. Today it is a haven for visitors who want a quiet (except in the high season), unspoilt island with beautiful sandy beaches in the south. The best way to explore Anáphi is either on foot or with a donkey inland, and by caique along the coast. Visit the **Venetian castle** and **ancient ruins** at Kastélli; and the **Monastery of Panagía tis Kalamiótissas**, where according to legend the Virgin's sacred icon was found hanging on a cane.

On many of the more remote islands, you will find seclusion on beautiful, sandy beaches, such as this one.

Information: There is a caique to Santoríni, whose erupting lava piled on top of Anáphi's original limestone. Some unsympathetic new building.

Port: Agios Nikólaos

Size: 38km² (14.7sq miles)

Population: 300

How to get there: By ferry from Piraeus

Connections: To Santoríni.

ÁNDROS

elegant squares – museums – nightlife – verdant landscape

Known as the 'ship-owner's island', the second largest of the Cyclades is atypical. Ándros does not have to rely on tourism for its income and Greeks say it is unfriendly as a result. The **Archaeological Museum** (with its Hermes of Ándros, said to be by Praxiteles) and the **Museum of Modern Art** – both endowed by the wealthy Goulandris ship-owning family – are well worth visiting in Hóra . There are frequent buses to most of the villages on the island. Inland are the impregnable **Monastery of Falika** (10C); the **Spring of Dionysos** at Menites, where water became wine; and the eerie **Cave of Chaos** at Aladino.

Small fishing boats tied to a rock jetty on Ándros, with the modern village of Batsi in the distance.

The wines of Ándros are good. The island's own drink is *soumada*: milky, bitter-sweet and made from almonds. Also try the sausages and the soft cheese with pepper, *kopanisti*.

Information: The easily accessible beaches tend
   to be crowded with Athenian weekenders,
   who also create a lively nightlife in Hóra.
Port: Gávrio
Size: 380km² (146sq miles)
Population: 9 000
How to get there: By ferry from Rafína to Gávrio
   harbour (2 to 4 services daily).

ANTÍPAROS (ANDÍPAROS)
(see also PÁROS)

quiet sandy coves – windsurfing – a mysterious cave

On the way to Agios Georgios with its
secluded beaches of fine sand, the principal
tourist attraction is a **great cave** full of eerie
stalactites and stalagmites. Here the
islanders used to hide during Moorish and
Turkish raids, and in 1673 the highly
eccentric (some might say mad) French
Ambassador to Constantinople, the Marquis
de Nointel, held a Christmas service before

The island inhabitants are usually very welcoming to tourists.

23

a massive stalagmite known as the 'Holy Altar'. The church at the entrance to the cave is known as 'St John of the Cave' (Agíou Ioánni tou spilióti). Although Antíparos tends to attract day trippers from its much larger sister island during the high season, it still remains a peaceful place. Try the local wines.

A local couple bang squid against the harbour wall to tenderize them.

Information: Antíparos is adjacent to Páros (*see* p.42) and also has three small islands close by: Despotikó has ruins from the Cycladic period; Saliagos is where archaeological remains have also been found; and Revmatonissi is a private island owned by the Goulandris ship-owning family.

Port: Antíparos (from Páros)

Size: 35km² (13½sq miles)

Population: 650

How to get there: Daily by caique from Páros in season.

Connections: *See* Páros.

DELOS (DÍLOS)
(see *also* **MYKONOS**)

sacred ruins at heart of the Cyclades – birthplace of Apollo (the sun) – Artemis (the moon) – and Hecate (death)

In a half-hour sea trip from the tourist centre of Mykonos to desolate, uninhabited Delos, visitors can journey back in time to classical antiquity and beyond that to the world of myths. Coming round the northern tip of Delos the ferry passes the island of Rínia, where the goddess Artemis, virgin huntress and twin sister of Apollo was born, and another islet, Revmatiaris, where the hideous goddess of Death, Hecate herself, first came among mortals.

As the traditional birthplace of the sun god Apollo, Delos became an important shrine at a very early date. It was already flourishing during the Mycenaean era, and around 1000 BC Homer describes the 'long-robed Ionians' honouring Apollo on Delos. The excellent harbour encouraged trade as well as pilgrimage. Merchants from Egypt and Syria were so numerous that they imported their own deities. For example, visit The Terrace of the Foreign Gods, at the foot of Mount Kynthos. If you have the time, climb to the summit; it is not difficult. From here, you can see most of the islands of the Cyclades. This is at the very centre of the Ancient Greek World; only the oracle at Delphi on the mainland can rival Delos in importance. The top of Mount Kynthos is where Zeus watched Leto give birth to his son.

On first leaving the ferry, turn left into the **Sanctuary** (Hieron). Of special interest are the Sanctuary of Apollo and the Sanctuary of Artemis, behind which is the colossal, shattered statue of Apollo.

Then make your way to the Lion District and the splendid **Lion Terrace** (one was plundered by the Venetians and now sits above the Arsenal). This faces the Sacred Lake where Leto endured her nine-hour labour, alone and clinging to a palm tree.

Passing behind the lake (now drained) where Apollo's sacred swans once lived, you come to the excellent **Museum**. Afterwards, see the **House of Hermes** (whose head you will have seen in the Museum) and the **Terrace of the Foreign Gods**. If not climbing Mount Kynthos, look out for the **House of Masks** with its magnificent mosaic of Dionysus, and the **House of Dolphins**, before making your way back to the dock through the **Theatre District** with its magnificent mansions.

A visit to the impressive Lion Terrace of Delos to see the five remaining marble statues is a must.

Information: The regular caique from Mykonos will give you only three hours on the island, returning at 1pm. This is not long enough to do justice to Delos and there is no accommodation on the island except for museum staff. You may find more flexible boats or consider hiring one as a group. It is a good idea to take your own picnic.

Size: 3km^2 (1sq mile)
Population: 16
How to get there: Boat from Mykonos (Note: the sea is usually rather rough)
Connections: *See* Mykonos.

DONOÚSSA AND MINOR ISLANDS (KOUPHONÍSSI – SCHINOÚSSA – IRÁKLIA)

Between Náxos and Amorgós are six minor islands which we will look at as a group. In an arc running roughly north-east to south-west, from the top these are Donoússa (separated from the rest); Kouphoníssi (two islets); Kéros; Shinoússa and Iráklia. All the islands are unspoilt and undeveloped, with basic facilities only. Each has its own character.

The sea crossing to the island of Donoússa from Amorgós is often rough. When it is very rough there are often cancellations which increases the isolation of a place which, in any case, has fewer connections than its neighbours. Donoússa is a wild, rocky island, parched under the sun. The clear sandy coves and rocks for snorkelling are the main attraction, but shade is scarce. The only way to explore is on foot or by caique. There are some prehistoric ruins and several tiny churches. By boat you can also find the **Seal Cave** (Phokospília), where the Mediterranean seal (*Monachus monachus*) was once king.

Information: There are approximately 100 rooms for visitors (varying standards, mostly basic), and a handful of tavernas. There is no bank. This is not the destination for those wanting luxury or nightlife but as a get-away-from-it-all island it is hard to beat. Try the local sweet red wine and the fiery *raki* distilled on the island.

Port: Stavros
Size: 36km² (14sq miles)
Population: under 200
How to get there: From Amorgós.

Kouphoníssi (Koufoníssi)

There are two islands: Páno (Upper) and Káto (Lower) Kouphoníssi, separated by a 200-m (650-ft) channel. The fishing is excellent, supports a thriving community, attracts knowledgeable visitors (especially from Greece) and ensures that the tavernas are well stocked with delicious seafood. Káto Kouphoníssi is practically uninhabited except in the season when a taverna is opened. The best beach is Phinikas on Páno Kouphoníssi.

Information: Finding a room may sometimes be a problem in the high season. There is no bank.
Size: 20km² (7.7sq miles)
Port: Koufoníssi
Population: 250
How to get there: From Amorgós.

Schinoússa (Shinoússa)

It is a hard life on this little island, which supports itself by traditional agriculture. But the people are friendly and generally as unspoilt as their island home. Many of the girls are called Akathí, after the church Panagía tis Akathís (the Standing Madonna) in the village of Schinoússa. The little

This local priest enjoying Antíparos harbour presents an interesting contrast with his sunglasses and long white beard.

church in Messariá (Theotokou) has an even more evocative dedication. 'She who gave birth to God'. Just beyond Messariá is perhaps the best of many beaches: Psilí Ammos, meaning 'fine sand'.

Information: No bank, no police, no public transport, no disco. Do not be put off by the miserable climb from the dock to the main settlement, Schinoússa. There are approximately 60 rooms available for visitors.

Size: 25km² (9.7sq miles)

Population: under 200

How to get there: Near enough to Iráklia for caique trip.

Iráklia

This is the least developed of all the occupied
islands in the group. As the ferry approaches
the port you will see the little island of
Venetiko with its Venetian castle which once
guarded the approach. Homer, writing
around 1000 BC, records that little Iráklia
provided 20 ships for the war with Troy. It is
hard to imagine the island as it must have
been then. Today it is a quiet, sleepy place
with a few simple tavernas. Visitors usually
stay either close to the delightful port of
Ágios Giórgios or at nearby **Livadi Beach**.
Both have sandy beaches with crystal-clear
water, or there is the more remote Tou
Korigadou beach further down the coast. On
the far side of the island is a cave which a
local guide will be pleased to take you to see,
preferably by caique. On the eve of St John's
Day (28 August) the islanders celebrate Mass
among the stalactites and stalagmites.

Information: There are approximately 40 rooms
for visitors. No bank, post office or public
transport.
Port: Ágios Giórgios
Size: 55km² (21sq miles)
Population: under 100
How to get there: Ferry from Piraeus.

ÍOS

*throbbing nightlife – nudist beaches – young people
from all over the world – Homer's tomb*

On a voyage from Sámos to Athens, Homer
– perhaps realizing that he was dying – asked
for the ship to pull in to Íos, his mother's
island. Fortunately for the old poet it is a
good 3-hour walk (or a long donkey trek or
caique trip) from Hóra to his tomb at the
north of the island. Otherwise his 3 000-year

rest might be disturbed by the vigorous
nightlife which has youth from Sydney and
Paris, Berlin and New York dancing the
night away throughout the summer months.

There are also some very good beaches,
but those looking for a quiet time and those
offended by naked flesh would do better to
visit another island. Food is not really the
priority on Íos, but its nutritious cheese
(*ksinotiri*) and the superb local honey may
help you to keep dancing 'til dawn.

Information: In August there is an international
   festival of live music.
Port: Gialos
Size: 109km² (42sq miles)
Population: 1 500
How to get there: By ferry daily from Piraeus. Many
   services daily in season.
Connections: Ferry to
   Santoríni, Síkinos and
   Folégandros.

*Shepherds are still
part of the daily
scene on many of
the Greek islands.*

KÉA
*groves of oak trees – small yachts
– a stone lion – quiet villages*

Although it is the closest
of all the Cycladic islands
to Athens, Kéa –
sometimes called Tzía –
has a life apart from
tourism. The yachts and
apartments of weekenders
are restricted to one or
two coastal sites, while the
interior concerns itself
with olives, almonds and
sheep farming. The great
oak forests are the gift of
Aristaeos, son of Apollo,

31

who petitioned Zeus to send the cool
breezes known as *meltémia*. In classical times,
Kéa was famous for the local custom of
committing suicide by drinking hemlock
after reaching the age of 70.

Ioulís (Hóra) is built on the northern
slopes of the mountain called after the
Prophet Elias. There are magnificent views
of the islands and the coast of Attica from
the acropolis. A short walk to the north-east
of Ioulís is the *Lion of Kéa*: an impressive
sculpture cut from the living rock in the
6C BC.

Information: In tavernas, look out for the local
speciality, *paspala*: a pork dish, cooked with
eggs and tomatoes.
Port: Korissía
Size: 131km² (50sq miles)
Population: 1 700
How to get there: By ferry daily from Lávrio.
By hydrofoil from Piraeus.

KÍMOLOS (see also MELOS)

*lava stone cottages – thermal springs – a fortified tower
– goat tracks*

Long famous for its unique *kimolite* chalk
deposits used in the manufacture of
porcelain, Kímolos did not until recently
have to think about tourism. As a result it is
largely unspoilt, offering opportunities for
visitors who like to explore. Hóra (called
Horió locally) has a fine **fortified tower**
(*kástro*). The adventurous can follow the
goat tracks to Paleókastro, a glowering
Venetian fortress. Look out for the local
dish, a proto-pizza called *ladenia*, dough in a
shallow pan, covered with olive oil, tomatoes
and onions and baked in the oven. (*Ladi*
means oil in Greek).

Information: Kímolos has a limited number of
  beds and can be quiet even in the high season.
Port: Psathí
Size: 36km² (13.9sq miles)
Population: 790
How to get there: From Melos.

KYTHNOS (KÍTHNOS)

healing waters – a secret school – barren landscape

Even by the standards of the Cyclades,
Kythnos is barren, yet recent excavations
indicate that this may have been one of the
first islands to be occupied by man. In
classical times it was much more heavily
populated and famous for its good
administration (Aristotle mentioned the
State of Kythnos).

Hóra is 6km (4 miles) from the port. The
monastery of Panagía tou Níkous has a
secret school (*Krifo Scholio*) in its cellars.
During the 400 years of Ottoman occu-
pation, the teaching of Greek was forbidden.
Children were sent at night to have lessons
in hidden rooms in churches and monasteries to keep Greek culture alive.

To the north of Hóra are the famous
thermal baths at Loutrá. The waters of this
spa are said to be good for arthritis and
eczema, as well as infertility. To the south is a
beautiful walk to Dhriopída, once the
capital, with its renowned **cave** (the Katafíki)
where a mass is held on Easter Day.

Information: Visitors are mainly Athenians.
  Kythnos is a quiet, friendly island with some
  reasonably good beaches. The local basket-
  work is very good. Also try the sausages, hard
  cheese *tirovolia*, and white wine *retsina*, which
  has a unique flavour.
Port: Mérihas

Size: 100km² (38sq miles)
Population: 1 500
How to get there: By ferry, daily service from
Piraeus; from Lávrio three days a week.
Connections: Ferry to Sériphos, Síphnos and
Melos.

MELOS (MÍLOS)
(see also KÍMOLOS)

*marine caves used by pirates – Christian catacombs –
rare minerals – the 'Venus de Milo'*

Melos has one of the best natural harbours
in the Aegean, large enough to shelter the
allied fleet during World War I. The skills of
its pilots were legendary; it was often Melian
navigators at the helm of the great ships of
the Venetian fleet. The pirates who preyed
on the fleet were also sometimes from Melos
and the **marine caves** in which they hid are
one of the wonders of the island. Particularly
spectacular are the Papafranga Caves on the
northern coast, the Emerald Cave (Sikia),
and Thalassina Meteora in the south. There
is an excursion from Adámas.

The island's rich deposits of obsidian – a
rare black igneous rock from which very
sharp weapons and tools could be made –
attracted interest as long as 5 000 years ago.
The Archaeological Museum in Athens has
many interesting exhibits from Melos's long
history, including a copy of the *Venus de Milo*
now in the Louvre. This masterpiece of
Hellenistic art from the 2C BC famously lost
her arms in the tug of war which followed
her discovery in 1820.

At the top of the town is I Panagía i
Thalassítra, a chapel on the site where the
Melians made their last stand against Athens
in 416 BC. At sunset you will have one of the
best **views** in the Aegean from here. In the

morning, you may be interested to visit the **catacombs** which lie about 1km (½ mile) to the south of the Pláka. This Christian burial place – containing more than 5 000 bodies in tunnels hollowed out of the rock – is the only one of its kind in Greece.

Information: Apolónia, on the northern tip, is noted for its windsurfing. Paleohóri is probably the best beach on the island, with volcanic vents heating the water, but is not easily accessible. Try the *pitarakía*, the local cheese pies and the excellent wines with wonderful flavours derived from the volcanic soil.

Port: Adámas

Size: 151km² (58sq miles)

Population: 4 600

How to get there: By air from Athens: 3 to 4 daily services in summer; 1 to 2 services in winter. By ferry from Piraeus: 1 to 2 services daily in summer; 1 in winter.

Connections: Ferries to Syros, Folégandros, Sikínos, Íos and Santoríni, which are less frequent services than the above.

MYKONOS (MÍKONOS)

narrow streets of the old town – 'Little Venice' – exotic and expensive nightlife – windmills – cruise ships – nudist beaches – watersports

Mykonos is the most cosmopolitan and expensive of all the Aegean islands. Direct flights from many countries and a huge influx of foreign tourists each year mean that the facilities and nightlife are

One of Mykonos' famous semi-tame pelicans poses for the camera.

second to none, and the months of July and August are extremely hectic for all but the most gregarious. Nevertheless, Mykonos is a very beautiful island, its old town one of the most picturesque in the Cyclades.

The island takes its name from the grandson of Apollo, Mykonos. It is said to be one of the rocks hurled against the Giants (*Gigantes*) by Poseidon in the Battle of the Gods. The chic bars and discos of the international set are only the latest outside influence which Mykonos has known in its long history. Egyptians, Phoenicians, Creteans, Ionians, Romans, Venetians,

There are many pleasant places to eat and drink in Mykonos. This is a traditional inn.

Turks, Russians and French (breaking the British blockade during the Napoleonic Wars by running wheat from the Black Sea) have all left their mark on the island. The colourful history of Mykonos is captured by the town's three exhibitions: the **Archaeological Museum**; the **Museum of Folk Art** and the **Aegean Maritime Museum**.

A rich nautical tradition goes hand-in-hand with a strong pirate tradition. It is said that the houses of **Little Venice** (Alefkándra) beyond the famous windmills were built with doors over the sea so that no-one could see the plunder being unloaded. The flower-decked streets of the **old town** (which are a delight to explore today) are said to have been made into a maze so that outside pirates would find it difficult to deprive Mykonos traders – legitimate or otherwise – of their bounty.

After climbing up to the **Boni Windmill** (Mílos Bóni) for a magnificent view across the sea to sacred Delos (especially at sunset) return to the interesting **harbour** via the little **Three Wells square** (Tría Pigádia). It is said

Fishermen untangling their nets at Mykonos harbour.

37

that if you drink the murky water you will find love on Mykonos (probably a nurse in the local hospital). Incidentally, Shirley Valentine found romance at the village of Agía Anna, some 12km (7½ miles) from the town.

The beautiful scenery of Mykonos from the thatch-topped windmills.

Information: Even if you are obliged to go in the high season, Mykonos is a must. There are many good beaches for all tastes, and activities include windsurfing, waterskiing, diving and snorkelling. Mykonos nightlife is sophisticated and caters for every possible taste. A different kind of wildlife can be enjoyed on an excursion to Tragoníssi, which is an idyllic islet with seals, seabirds and wonderful scenery.

Port: Mykonos

Size: 86km² (33sq miles)

Population: 5 500

How to get there: By air: from Athens daily services (8 in summer; 6 in winter); 3 a week from Herakleion, Thessalonika and Rhodes; and 1 from Santoríni. By ferry from Piraeus: daily morning service and several boats sailing in late afternoon during the week.

Connections: To neighbouring islands and Santoríni.

NÁXOS

*magnificent sandy beaches – green fertile valleys –
marble* koúri *(naked male figures) – delicious wine*

The largest and greenest island in the
Cyclades also has the highest peak at its
centre: Mount Zeus. On the approach to
Náxos Town (Hóra) by sea, visitors pass the
giant stone portal of the unfinished Temple
of Apollo. Built in the 6C BC, this marks the
legendary spot where Theseus abandoned
Ariadne. The worship of Dionysus, god of
wine and the harvest, was always important
on fertile Náxos. Visitors can still sample the
delicious vegetables and fruit, pungent
cheeses and scented Náxian wines which the
sensual god would have enjoyed – although
he might find the nightlife around the
harbour rather tame compared with his
dionysia. For a clearer picture of a Greek
god's idea of fun, visit the Archaeological
Museum with its mosaic of Zeus in the form
of a bull ravishing Europa.

*The giant stone
portal amidst the
ruins of the Temple
of Apollo at Náxos
Town.*

Relax and make merry at one of the many outdoor cafés.

Some holidaymakers find the island interior, and mountain villages, such as Apírathos, with its fierce Cretean traditions, rather forbidding, but it is well worth exploring. Here you will find **Fleríó**, whose marble quarries still contain unfinished male statues (*koúri*) from the 6C BC, abandoned because of flaws in the stone. At **Belónia** you can see houses fortified by the Venetians in a town once owned by the Roman Catholic bishops of Náxos. Further up the lush Potamiá Valley – crowded with orchards, vines and olive groves – is Halkí and a fine **Byzantine church** with interesting frescoes.

The marble of Náxos and the artists who shaped it were famous throughout the Ancient World. Close to the village of Apólonas in the north of the island, with its pleasant harbour and beach, is a **marble quarry** containing a *koúros* of immense size, still part of the rock from which it was carved in the 7C BC.

Information: 5km (3 miles) south of Náxos (Hóra) is Prokópios beach, and beyond that the white sands of tree-lined Pláka beach, considered by some the best on the island.

Port: Náxos

Size: 438km² (166sq miles)

Population 14 000

How to get there: By air from Athens: 1 service daily. By ferry from Piraeus: 3 to 6 services daily.

Connections: Ferries to Íos and Santoríni; Amorgós, Astipálea, Kálimnos; Síkinos, Folégandros; and Crete.

The men of the village Skado on Náxos tend to the vines on the terraced hillside.

PÁROS

Cycladic houses and Venetian mansions – nightlife – watersports – dazzling marble – butterflies.

Many visitors use Páros as a base from which to explore other islands. It has excellent ferry connections, and a busy cosmopolitan atmosphere which is invigorating to return to after some of the quieter destinations. The nightlife on Páros rivals that of Mykonos and is slightly less expensive. The island also has many opportunities for watersports, including surfing, and some excellent beaches. With all this it is not surprising that Páros can get overcrowded during July and August. Nevertheless, it is a beautiful island: domed churches, windmills and Christmas-cake houses, narrow shady alleys opening into little squares where flowers overflow the balconies.

A splendidly designed church stands out above the whitewashed houses at the village of Léfkes on Páros.

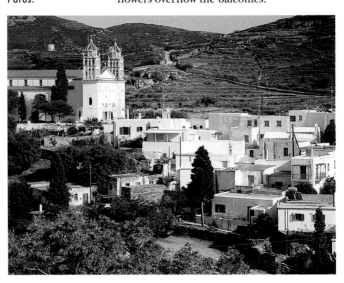

In classical times, Páros was famous for its lychnite, the pure white marble from which Praxiteles sculpted the *Venus de Milo* and *Hermes*, and which was used to clad the legendary Temple of Solomon in Jerusalem. Part of the famous Parian Chronicle – the history of Greece up to 264 BC carved in marble – can be seen at the **Archaeological Museum** in Páros Town (Parikía). Nearby is one of the most beautiful and interesting churches in the Aegean: **The Church of Our Lady of 100 Gates** (Panagía Ekatondapi-lianí). Founded by St Helen, the mother of Constantine, in the 4C on her pilgrimage to the Holy Land in search of the True Cross, it is full of interest. There is a legend that the architect of the 6C building, Isidore of Miletus, allowed his pupil Ignatius to com-plete the work. The result was so beautiful that the master attacked his brilliant pupil in a jealous rage, both plunging to their death from the roof.

There is a pleasant excursion south of Parikía to the **Convent of Christ in the Woods** (Hristós Dássous) and **Butterfly Valley** (Petaloúdes). In the summer months, the trees in this scented valley are covered by clouds of tiger moths.

In the centre of the island are the famous **marble quarries** (Latomía Marmárou). The galleries are cut deep into the mountain where the purest, finest stone – brilliant white and flawless – was found. It is pleasant to take a picnic and dream of all the wonders of the Ancient World – the palaces and statues in Athens, Rome, the Levant and Egypt – which had their origins here.

Information: Páros has a wonderful festival on 15 August each year when the fishing boats are decked with lanterns, and fireworks explode over the harbour. The white and rosé wines of Páros are delicious and the shellfish and sardines are famous. Also try the local lemon liqueur.

Port: Parikía

Size: 195km² (75sq miles)

Population: 8 000

How to get there: By air from Athens: 7 to 10 services daily in summer; 3 services daily in winter. By ferry: from Piraeus 3 to 7 services daily. From Rafína, daily service.

Connections: Ferry: daily to Náxos, Íos and Santoríni; 3 days a week to Amorgós; 3 days a week to Ikaría and Sámos, continuing 1 day a week to Síkinos and Folégandros, and to Crete.

SANTORÍNI (THERA – THÍRA)

astonishing scenery – dark volcanic beaches – luscious wines – the legend of Lost Atlantis

The approach to Santoríni from the sea is one of the great sights of the world. Visitors never forget the terrifying cliffs rising sheer out of the sea, enveloping the vulnerable ferry as it enters the caldera of the drowned volcano. The blue water is so deep it is impossible to drop anchor, and above the dark, lifeless cliff-face the white houses of the town cling precariously to the summit.

In this landscape, the line between history and myth becomes blurred. Is Santoríni the last remaining fragment of Atlantis, the lost civilization described by Plato? What is certain is that between 2000 and 1500 BC a sophisticated culture developed on Santoríni, probably linked to the civilization which then flourished on Minoan Crete. Around 1550 BC a cataclysm occurred. Gases beneath the volcanic island exploded, tearing a great crater out of its heart and sending ash and rock high into the atmosphere. The sea

White-coloured, stepped houses in the village of Ía, Santoríni, with a typical blue-domed church.

The imposing cliffs of Santoríni.

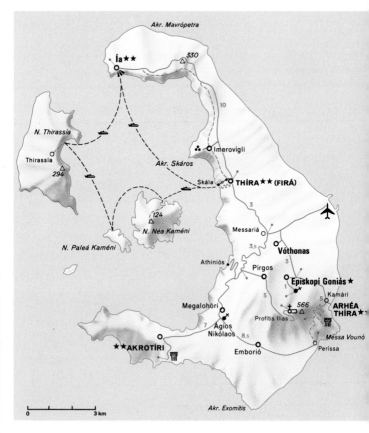

Map of Santoríni.

rushed into the chasm and a tidal wave
deluged Crete and the other islands. The ash
clouds made day into night, crops died and
famine ensued. Perhaps this was the Deluge
recorded in the Bible and in other ancient
accounts? We may never know. But we do
know it was the end of Minoan civilization.

During the zig-zag, donkey-back ascent
(there is now a cable-car) from Skála Firá
(other ferries land off Órmos Athiniós and
Ía) to **Thera Town** there is time to enjoy the
view and to decide where to stay and what to
see. Thera itself is expensive – especially if
you want a room with a view – and crowded.
The regular appearance of cruise ships has
encouraged the growth of souvenir shops
and the like, which has rather robbed Thera
of its soul. All this becomes much better out
of season. Thera nightlife is unremarkable,
especially when compared with the revels
enjoyed by the worshippers of Dionysus
which can be seen in the **Archaeological
Museum**.

The port of **Ía** in the north-west of the
island is a place full of character. From here
it is interesting to take a boat excursion to
Thirassía, which was split from the main
island in the 3C BC. The adventurous could

*Looking south along
the length of
Santoríni over the
rooftops of Thera
Town.*

47

also visit **Kaméni**: a satanic landscape of hot springs and sulphurous exhalations on an islet which rose from the abyss.

At the south-western tip of Santoríni is **Akrotíri**, where visitors can catch glimpses of the civilization destroyed in c.1550 BC. Most of the wonderful frescoes are now in Athens, but Akrotíri is still well worth a visit.

If the modern holiday development on the east of the island – at **Kamári Beach** and **Períssa Beach** – with their extraordinary black volcanic sand, are not to your liking, explore **Ancient Thera** (Arhéa Thíra). These ruins of a city which had 5 000 inhabitants at its peak in the 2C BC are extraordinary.

Excavations have revealed the temple walls at Ancient Thera.

Information: The luscious wines of Santoríni are legendary. Vegetables, and especially tomatoes, grown on the rich volcanic soil also have a unique flavour.

Ports: Ía; Skála Firá; Órmos Athiniós

Size: 76km² (29sq miles)

Population: 11 000

How to get there: By air: from Athens 3 to 7 services daily; in season daily service from Mykonos; 2 to 3 services a week from Herakleion and 3 to 4 services a week from Rhodes. By ferry from Piraeus: daily services (several in summer).

SÉRIPHOS (SÉRIFOS)

rugged walking – a classic hóra – the head of the Gorgon

Gold was mined on Sériphos in antiquity, and it is appropriate that it was here that the legendary hero Perseus was conceived after Zeus – in one of his more imaginative seductions – drenched Danoië in 'a shower of gold'.

Since the days of Perseus and his mother, life on Sériphos has become altogether quieter. There is accommodation at the port. From here you can explore **Hóra** with its Venetian castle. Sériphos is a good island for walkers, with sudden splashes of green where water gushes from the barren landscape. Explore the hundreds of uncharted tracks, or visit **Panagía** with its Byzantine church and views. The red-domed **monastery of the Taxiarchs**, near Galíni, is also interesting.

Information: Psilí Ámmos (east) or Sikamiá (north) are better beaches than Livadáki, near the port.

Port: Livádi

Size: 75km² (29sq miles)

Population: 1 100
How to get there: By ferry: daily (1 to 3 services in season) from Piraeus via Kythnos.
Connections: To Síphnos and Melos.

SÍKINOS

mule transport – quiet coves and beaches – a church built on a pagan temple

On Síkinos it is still possible to glimpse what life was like before tourism came to the Aegean. If you have ever wondered how 19C travellers fared when the only way to explore was on the back of a donkey, you can find out on Síkinos. The bus connects the port with Hóra and adjacent Kástro. This is the only road on the island.

Walkers may feel otherwise, but the best way to reach **Episkopí** – where a church has grown out of an ancient temple dedicated to Apollo – is by donkey. The track clings to the mountainside along the coast for nearly 4km (2½ miles) with spectacular views across the sea. Those not expert in donkey psychology would do better to take a guide.

Kástro, its 18C square designed to be defended, is a reminder of the pirate raids which were once a part of life. Locals will show you the bullet holes in the door of the 'Spring of Life' **monastery** (Zoodóhos Pigí) perched above the town.

Information: Try to find the sour milk cheese (*xino galo*) of the island. The local olive oil and honey is excellent, as is the bread. The best beach is probably Ágios Panteleimónas, south-west from the port (pebbles): caique in season. There is no bank.
Port: Aloprónia
Size: 41km² (15.8sq miles)
Population: 300
How to get there: From Piraeus.

SIPHNOS (SÍFNOS)

pottery – watersports – flower-decked tavernas – capers – a golden egg

This charming island is the ideal destination for those who like a place to be unspoilt – but not to the point of inconvenience. The islanders, who have a reputation for being reserved, have developed Siphnos for discerning tourists.

A travelling melon seller on Siphnos.

Kástro – the old capital, built on a headland – is a wonderful example of a fortified town. There is snorkelling and swimming on the rocky beaches below. **Apolonía** – dedicated to the sun god and built on three hills – is a perfect Cycladic town, waves of white houses rising from a barren landscape. It has many places to explore and good tavernas. There is a strong culinary tradition on Siphnos. In antiquity, Siphnos sent an annual tribute of a golden egg to the sacred oracle at Delphi. Try the cheese pies, perhaps with the famous capers grown on the island, and a glass of the local wine. Also good is *revithada*, chick peas cooked in a pot with spices and lemon. Close to Apolonía is **Artemónas**, full of interesting

The church of Taxiarkhis at Vathi on Siphnos.

houses and churches – one built on the site of a temple to Artemis.

The most popular beach is Platís Yialós. Another can be found at the quiet resort of Fáros.

Information: There is a good bus service. The local pottery and hand-woven fabrics are of excellent quality.
Port: Kamáres
Size: 73km² (28sq miles)
Population: 2 100
How to get there: By ferry from Piraeus daily (1 to 3 services daily according to the season).
Connections: To Melos. In summer, boat services to Páros.

SYROS (SÍROS)

an historic port – a miniature La Scala – loukoúmi
(Turkish Delight) – bouzoúki music

If the Aegean islands are your first experience
of Greece, Syros will give you a strong feeling
of the mainland, and of Greek history since
Independence. The great port of **Ermoúpoli**
– named after Hermes, god of commerce and
communication – was once considered as a
possible capital for the newly established
Greek kingdom. Ermoúpoli had its heyday in
the 19C, and that is the city you see today.
Here are the grand mansions of the wealthy
ship-owners and merchants whose enterprises
stretched to the four corners of the world,
and who now rest in equally grand
mausoleums in the cemetery. Notice the neo-
classical civic buildings in the huge square,
Platía Miaoúli, named after an admiral; the
Apollon Theatre modelled on La Scala is
nearby. All have an elegant sadness about
them, like a well-groomed gentleman who
knows that his time was long ago. In the early
evening, when the traditional promenade
(*perípato*) takes place, sit in one of the coffee
shops (*kafenía*) on Platía Miaoúli with a pre-
dinner *ouzo* or a *métrio*.

It is a long, interesting climb to **Áno Síros**,
the medieval Catholic quarter. Here, chapels
and convents are everywhere in the narrow
streets below the bishop's palace and St
George's Cathedral. From Áno Síros there is
a fine view of their 'new' town and the deep-
water harbour beyond.

With the opening of the Corinth Canal in
1893, Ermoúpoli began its long decline,
supplanted gradually by Piraeus. The spirit
of this time – joyful and sad – is expressed in
rembetika music with its bouzoúki accompani-
ment. There are many bouzoúki bars in

Ermoúpoli and around the island. If you explore Syros you will find the beach resorts Galissás and Delagrazzia (Possidonía), both immortalized in song by the bouzoúki virtuoso Markos Vamvakaris.

Information: Syros is famous for its delicious *Loukoúmi* (Turkish Delight).
Port: Ermoúpoli
Size: 85km² (33sq miles)
Population: 20 000
How to get there: By air from Athens: 1 to 2 services daily. By ferry: from Piraeus frequent services daily, and from Rafína.
Connections: Ferry to Tenos and Mykonos, or Páros, Náxos, Íos and Santoríni (and occasionally to Sikínos and Folégandros or Amorgós); some services to Melos.

TENOS (TÍNOS)
the holiest shrine – dovecotes – folk art – the cruiser Elli

Tenos has a very special place in the Greek heart. First, it is the Holy island of the Greek Orthodox Church, sacred to the Virgin Mary, whose icon performs miracles. Thousands of pilgrims visit Tenos on 25 March (Annunciation) and 15 August (Assumption) each year. The faithful kneel in the streets, all the way from the port to the white marble church of Panagía on a hilltop, while the icon is carried over them.

Closely identified with this adoration of the Virgin Mary in the Greek psyche – since the act took place on the 15 August – was the sinking of the *Elli* in 1940. The Greek light cruiser lay at anchor off Tenos when it was torpedoed by an Italian submarine. The two countries were not at war. When war was declared – on 28 October – the Greeks were all the more determined to halt the Italian advance.

Tenos was a place of pilgrimage in antiquity. Visit the **Sanctuary of Poseidon** in **Kióna**, which also has a pleasant – but crowded – beach. Sculpture from the site can be seen in the **archaeological museum** in Tenos Town, which also has an extraordinary example of the dovecotes or pigeon towers which cover the island.

Information: Marble artefacts of all kinds are made on the island.
Port: Tenos
Size: 195km² (75sq miles)
Population: 7 800
How to get there: By ferry: daily service from Piraeus and Rafína.
Connections: Daily services to Mykonos and Syros.

Many Greek family names begin with 'papa', meaning 'priest'.

THE DODECANESE

Taking their name from the 12 main islands
which form the group (*dodeca* means 12),
these are the most distant of the Aegean
islands. The Dodecanese lie close to the
Turkish mainland; they were only made part
of the modern Greek state in 1948 after many
centuries of foreign domination by Romans,
Saracens, Venetians, Genoese, Algerians,
Arabs, the Knights of St John, Turks and, most
recently, Italians. Yet, for all the other cultural
influences, the Dodecanese have known they
are most decidedly Greek. From these islands
came Hippocrates, the 'father of medicine';
Erinna, the first woman poet; Xenophon,
Apelles, Anthias and many more. Modern
Dodecanesians, despite their turbulent and
often tragic history, are warm and friendly.
Their islands are generally less barren than
the Cyclades, and many more of them are
completely unspoiled. From the main tourist

*The Dodecanese
islands are often
more fertile than
the Cyclades.*

centres of Rhodes and Kos it is quite easy to visit islands where the 20C seems like an improbable dream. But read the guide carefully, there are still places with no electricity, no running water, no shop – unless, of course, that is what you want.

ASTIPÁLEA

caves – legends – a fine castle – a disgraced Olympian

Ironically, the first of the Dodecanese (alphabetically) is more like a Cycladic island: a barren, sun-scorched landscape; a white-washed town (*hóra*) surmounted by a Venetian castle. Astipálea is really two islands (Mésa Nisí, the eastern half; Óxo Nisí, the western) joined by a narrow isthmus to form a butterfly shape. The settlement on the isthmus, Análipsi, is also known as Maltesána because of Maltese pirate raids in the past. You will find some beaches here, although these are not the island's strong point. More interesting are the Roman baths and mosaics.

The eastern half of the island is of less interest. The Dragon's Cave on the northern tip involves a caique trip through dangerous waters best left to the dragon. The Caves of the Moor (Spília Negroú) on the south coast of the western island are more interesting. Before the Moorish pirate hid his booty and victims there, Christians may have hid from Roman persecutors (skeletons and an altar have been found). More recently, British World War II commandos used the caves to hide from the Germans.

The town is the main attraction of the island. The houses – many of them owned by foreigners – are beautifully kept. Below the castle is the delightful **church of Panagía tis Portaítissas**. The **Venetian castle** is one of the most impressive in the Aegean. Built by the

Quirini family in the 13C, it once housed the entire town of several thousand souls within its fortified walls. Remnants of massive masonry suggest that this was the site of the ancient acropolis. In antiquity, this was the scene of a notorious incident which shows that Olympic tantrums and athletes being sent home in disgrace are nothing new. Kleomedes – disqualified for killing an opponent in a wrestling contest – was so incensed by his homecoming that he tore down the school in Astipálea, killing all the children.

Information: The best places to eat are Skála and Livádi. There is a bus service and mopeds everywhere.
Port: Skála
Size: 97km² (37½sq miles)
Population: 1 100
How to get there: Ferry via Amorgós or Kálimnos.

HÁLKI
a castle of the Knights of St John – UNESCO – views of Turkey and the Dodecanese
Designated 'the Isle of Peace and Friendship' by UNESCO in the 1980s, as part of a scheme to rebuild the old harbour area and make the island a venue for youth conferences, Hálki is now largely dependent upon tourism. The sponges which were once the mainstay of the economy began to die off early this century, causing large-scale migration of the islanders to Rhodes and America.

There are some good beaches at Póndamos (sandy) and Dío Yialí (pebbles) both near the pleasant port. But the main attraction of the island is deserted **Horió** dominated by a castle built on the site of the ancient acropolis by the Knights of St John.

Information: Look for the local speciality *oftó*:
   lamb stuffed with liver and rice.
Port: Hálki
Size: 20km² (7.7sq miles)
Population: 350
How to get there: From Rhodes
Connections: From Rhodes.

KÁLIMNOS

sponges – a bustling port – cool groves in a barren landscape

The approach to Kálimnos is memorable: elegant pastel-coloured houses and churches jostle for position on the hillside behind the busy quay. During the war many islanders took to painting their houses blue and white – the colours of the Greek flag – in order to annoy the Italians. Many tourists on day trips from Kos and Rhodes make straight for the workshops preparing the sponges for which Kálimnos is famous. There are still bargains to be had,

The serene village of Póthia on Kálimnos.

Kálimnos is well known for its sponge factories.

although sadly fewer and fewer of the sponges are provided by local boats and divers, because of blight in the Aegean.

Mirtiés and Massoúri cater mainly for package holidays, but a boat trip from there to the volcanic islet **Télendos** for lunch and a swim can be fun. From the main port there are interesting excursions to sea caves, or you can visit the lush valley of Vathis.

Information: The best tavernas are around the port. Look for octopus and *mouoúri*, stuffed lamb.
Port: Póthia
Size: 93km² (35sq miles)
Population: 15 000
How to get there: Day excursions from Kos Town. Also ferry from Piraeus.

KÁRPATHOS

secluded beaches – women in traditional dress –
a strange custom – magnificent coastal scenery

Kárpathos was first colonized by Creteans and
then Myceneans. You stumble across relics of
antiquity everywhere. The southern part of
the island is more developed for tourism,
although all of Kárpathos is surprisingly
unspoilt. There are numerous rocky bays and
sandy coves on the east coast – north of the
main port – best reached by caique.

The port, sometimes known as Pigádia
(wells), is largely modern. But ancient
customs survive. During Lent a 'people's
court' is held to judge men who have
committed immoral acts. On that day men
dress as women, with much ribald comment.
After arrest by *tzafiedes* (gendarmes) the
accused are tried, convicted and sentenced
to do silly things.

The north has preserved even more of its
ancient culture – many women wear the
traditional costume – although change will
accelerate with the improvement of the port
of Diaphani. At Ólimbos, high on a dramatic
ridge, they speak a dialect with traces of
Homeric Greek.

Information: Island roads are very bad.
   Wherever possible travel by boat.
Port: Kárpathos Town (Pigádia)
Size: 301km^2 (116sq miles)
Population: 5 000
How to get there: By air from Rhodes; by ferry
   from Crete.

KÁSOS (KÁSSOS)

crumbling genteel houses – walking – seabirds

In days gone by, the sea captains and
navigators of Kásos were famous. The Turks

put the island to the sword in 1824 because of the vital part the islanders played in the revolutionary Greek navy. Until nationalization under Nasser, many of the Suez Canal pilots were Kásos men. The very name of the islands probably comes from the Phoenician word for 'foam'. Visitors are in safe hands if they take the boat to the islet of Armathía to find the best beach.

Most of the island is accessible only on foot. It is a 15-minute walk from the port to the capital Phri, so-named because the bay is like an eyebrow (*phridi*).

Information: Try the local dishes *paspara* (liver cooked with rice and raisins) and for dessert *ksikopita* (sweet cheese with honey).

Port: Emboriós

Size: 66km² (25.5sq miles)

Population: 1 200

How to get there: By air from Rhodes; by boat from Crete.

KOS

castles – high-rise hotels – Hippocrates – nightlife – beaches – red hibiscus – minarets and palm trees

This is one of the most popular holiday destinations in the Dodecanese. In Kos Town the ancient monuments are nearly as numerous as the visitors: pillars lie around like sunbathers. Only the grim Hospitaler's castle – still at its post guarding the harbour – keeps aloof from the pagan revelry. In the centre of the town, in **Plane Tree Square** (Platía tou Platánou), is the ancient tree under which the island's most famous son, Hippocrates, is said to have taught.

Also associated with the Father of Medicine are the ruins of the **Asklepieion**. Here, in a wonderful position – with uplifting scenery,

The ancient Roman Odeon near Casa Romana, a large Roman villa at Kos Town.

Map of Kos.

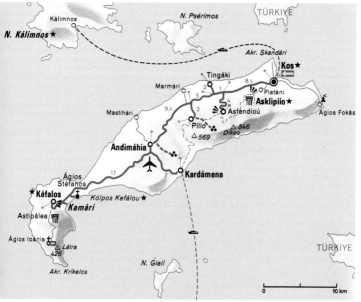

An old mosque in Kos is a reminder of the island's history.

spring water and scented air – followers of Hippocrates dispensed a curiously modern form of healing. You reach Asklipiío from the road which runs the length of the island. At the far south-western tip of Kos, beyond further castles and the airport, is **Kéfalos** the ancient capital. Nearby is **Kamári**, and a beach so beautiful that even the modern development cannot spoil its charm.

Information: For a more secluded beach at the north-eastern end try Brós Thermá, with its black sand and natural hot springs. A pleasant excursion – or even overnight visit – can be made to the delightful islet of **Psérimos**. Accommodation may be difficult in high season. Kos wine is sweet and fragrant. Also try the 'red' cheese coloured with wine.

Port: Kos
Size: 290km² (112sq miles)
Population: 21 000

How to get there: By air: from Athens 2 to 3
services daily (1 to 2 in winter); from Rhodes
2 to 3 services a week. By boat: from Piraeus
daily ferry service (6 a week in winter).

Connections: Daily ferry to Rhodes. Services to
Turkey in summer.

LÉROS

*walking – tree-lined boulevards – the Temple of
Artemis*

Léros looks as if great bites have been taken
out of its coastline. One of these at Lakkí, was
used as a naval base by the Italians during the
last war. The Art Deco buildings and
eucalyptus trees are a reminder of those
times. Despite its history as a place of exile
and detention, with still many medical
institutes on the island, Léros is friendly and
welcoming. It is ideal for those happy to
spend their time walking and enjoying
views. There are reasonable beaches at
Koúlouki near the port and at Vromólithos
close by the capital, Plátanos. There is a
Hospitaler's castle in the capital and some
fine 19C mansions. The **Temple of Artemis**,
to whom the island is sacred, is worth
exploring at Ksirókambos in the north.

Information: Take mosquito precautions.
Port: Lakkí
Size: 53km² (20.5sq miles)
Population: 8 200
How to get there: By air from Athens. By boat
from Piraeus.
Connections: By ferry to Sími, Tílos, Nísiros and
Lípsos.

LIPSÍ

To the east of Pátmos are some unspoilt
untouched, islands for those determined to

leave the 20C behind. Lipsí is the most fertile – its wine was once shipped to the Vatican for communion. It has a hotel as well as rooms. There are some beautiful sandy coves and, relatively, quite a few tourists.

Information: Visit Kasadiá cove with its taverna.
Port: Lipsí
Size: 21km² (8sq miles)
Population: 650.

NÍSSIROS

a volcanic crater – a sighing Titan –
a spectacular castle

During the War of the Gods, Poseidon threw part of Kos at the Titan Polybates, crushing him beneath it. When you visit the **crater** you can hear the trapped Titan hissing and moaning beneath your feet. Polybates last erupted in 1522, but he is still not a happy giant (nor a very sweet-smelling one).

Visitors will find accommodation in the capital Mandráki, or at the fishing village of Páli along the coast to the east. (Here and beyond are the best beaches.) Make a point of visiting **Paleókastro**, a magnificent defence built on massive foundations.

Information: Look out for the local almond drink *soumada*.

*(Previous page, left)
An awesome
volcanic crater on
Níssiros.*

*(Previous page,
right)
Crystals formed by
the action of steam
forcing its way
through the earth's
crust.*

Port: Mandráki
Size: 41km² (15.8sq miles)
Population: 950
How to get there: Excursions by boat from Kos.

PÁTMOS

*the Cave of the Apocalypse – St John's Monastery –
cruise ships – walking – beaches*

It was on this sacred island that St John the
Divine heard the voice of God dictating the
powerful message and unforgettable
imagery of the prophetic poem we call the
Apocalypse: 'I am the Alpha and the Omega,
the Beginning … and the End.'

Skála, where the boats dock, is a smart,
impersonal tourist centre. But visiting **St
John's Monastery** – its dark countenance
rising above a white collar made by the
houses of Hóra – is worth any inconvenience.
Standing on the site of a temple to Artemis –
said to have been built by Orestes while
fleeing the Furies – the 900-year-old
monastery is one of Christianity's most
important sites, a treasure house of religious
art, relics and books. It is a pleasant walk from
Hóra to the Convent of the Apocalypse where
St John heard God's voice 'like a trumpet'.

Information: When visiting all churches and
monasteries in Greece, modest dress is
mandatory (*see* Etiquette p.116).
Port: Skála
Size: 34km² (13sq miles)
Population: 2 600
How to get there: By air: via Léros (from Athens
1 service daily in summer, 5 services a week in
winter) or via Kos, and continuing by boat.
By boat: daily ferry service from Piraeus.
Connections: Ferry to Léros, Kálimnos and Kos.
In summer to Sámos.

SÍMI

*preserved mansions – juniper groves and cypress trees –
deep inlets – fortelling the future – excursion boats –
a famous monastery*

During the season, excursion boats from
Rhodes come to visit the impressive main
town of Sími, with its magnificent neo-
classical mansions and stepped way (*kalí
stráta*) joining the port, Egialós, to Hóra.
Once Sími rivalled Rhodes in wealth – even
in population – but building fine wooden
ships and supplying sponges to the baths
and harems of Turkey are no longer viable
industries.

If you stay on the island – and accommodation is not easy to come by – visit the
famous **Panormítis Monastery** in the south
(many excursion boats also stop there).
Visitors can stay in the pilgrim rooms
(*ksenónas*), for a small donation, and enjoy

*The harbour at
Sími.*

The church tower of the famous 18C Panormítis Monastery on Sími.

the museum. On the beach below is a touching memorial to the abbot and two other Greek patriots shot for helping British commandos in World War II.

Information: Do not be put off by the tourist development which day trips inevitably bring – Sími has more to offer. There are clean pebble beaches at the head of most of the island's deep inlets.
Port: Egialós
Size: 54km² (20.8sq miles)
Population: 2 200
How to get there: Daily boat services from Rhodes.

TÍLOS

a scattering of Hospitaler castles – groves of cypress, plane and poplar – pygmy elephants – peaceful beaches

A beautiful island for walking, with barren heights and green well-watered creases in the landscape. There are pebble beaches and some with volcanic sand, all to be discovered. Skeletons of 10 000-year-old pigmy elephants were found near the castle of Misariás, and human remains in the lava beach at Ágios Andónios trapped – Pompeii fashion – during a volcanic eruption from neighbouring Níssiros in 600 BC. At that time Tílos was populous and wealthy, even minting its own coinage.

The port is the best place for visitors. There is accommodation and it is well served with tavernas.

Information: A bus service to Megálo Horió (large village) coincides with ferry arrivals (usually).
Port: Livádia
Size: 63km² (24sq miles)
Population: 350
How to get there: Ferry from Rhodes.

THE SPORADES

The islands of this group are the 'scattered ones' (hence *diaspora*). Their geographic position, at the crossroads of the Aegean off the coast of Thessaly and Évia, has greatly influenced their history. The earliest settlement, on Alónissos, dates from around 7000 BC. The islands were later colonized by Minoans and then Myceneans. During the Classical period they were allied to Athens and helped repulse the mighty Persian Empire. The Sporades declined in importance after ruthless suppression by Rome, and were used as places of banishment by the Byzantines. The later history followed that of the mainland.

Today, the Sporades (or more correctly, the Northern Sporades) are holiday islands first and foremost with few historical sites to lure tourists away from the beaches, tavernas, bars and nightclubs.

ALÓNISSOS

a rocky coastline – protected wildlife – the cave of the Cyclops

In some respects, the most remote of the Sporades has never quite recovered from its

Restored houses on the southern coast of Alónissos.

A view towards Mourtia beach with old Alónissos in the far distance.

two modern disasters: Phyloxera, which destroyed its vines in the 1950s, and the earthquake of 1965. The population is now concentrated in Patitíri (named after the place where grapes are trodden). Despite its evocative name, it is a modern and largely concrete settlement. The old town (Hóra) of **Alónissos** is more attractive, although **Stení Vála**, half way up the northern coast, is a better place to stay. The villages in the north of the island provide peace and quiet but the sea currents all around are dangerous. There are an estimated 30 rare and en-dangered Mediterranean monk seals living

73

in the waters around Alónissos. They breed on the rocky offshore islets. Other protected species are dolphins, hawks and the wild goats of **Gioúra**. It is worth making an excursion by caique to this island, although one example of wildlife it would be better not to encounter is the Cyclops, Polyphemus, whose cave you can explore.

Information: The local lobster is delicious.
Port: Patitíri
Size: 64km² (25sq miles)
Population: 1 600
How to get there: Ferries from mainland Greece; in summer, excursions to and from Skópelos.

SKÍATHOS
beautiful, often crowded beaches – music and dancing – watersports – a fine monastery

For the gregarious and energetic, Skíathos is the idea holiday destination. In Skíathos Town there is music from Classical to Blues and food from Spanish to curry. (More

Decorative plates adorn the walls of this church on Skíathos.

Watch the world go by at one of the lively bars in Skíathos Town.

traditional is the local cheese pie, *tirópita*). It is a good-natured, lively place but not – on the face of it – particularly Greek.

There is another Skíathos if you look for it. The beautiful **Evangelístria Monastery** is where the general and hero of the Greek War of Independence, Theodoros Kolokotronis, took an oath to free Greece in

One of the more populated beaches of the islands.

1807. Here the first Greek flag – a white cross on a sea-blue background – was made. On the remote northern coast visitors can explore the old capital, **Kástro**, with its spectacular views (look for boat trips). There are also donkey excursions to the 15C **ruined monastery** Panagía tis Keriás, with its bat colony.

Information: There are boat excursions around the island, and water taxis to the famous **Lalária Beach** (dangerous undertow, *see* p.104) and Agía Eléni (also accessible by bus). There is windsurfing at Vromólinos and several good beaches nearby.

Port: Skíathos

Size: 50km² (19sq miles)

Population: 4 500

How to get there: By air: daily in summer from Athens; 3 a week from Thessalonika; 4 a week in winter from Athens. By boat: ferries from mainland Greece.

Connections: To Skyros.

SKYROS (SKÍROS)

'immortal poetry' – Achilles and Theseus – woodcarving – traditional costume – miniature horses

This beautiful island is full of surprises and interesting associations. In Skyros Town (Hóra) Theseus died, pushed from the summit of the rock on which it is built. Here the legendary warrior Achilles had his unhappy childhood, until – from the bay of Ahili down the coast – he sailed for the Trojan War. It was on a French hospital ship in Tris Boúkes Bay, on the eve of sailing for the Dardanelles in 1915, that the poet Rupert Brooke died. It was Brooke's wish that his 'corner of a foreign field' should be Skyros. You can reach his grave by road, but the boat from Linariá is better.

A memorial statue to the poet Rupert Brooke who is buried on Skyros.

The nude **memorial statue** to Rupert Brooke in Skyros Town – 'immortal poetry' – scandalized the local matrons when it was unveiled in 1930. Nearby, and less controversial, is an excellent **folk museum**. The handicrafts of Skyros are deservedly famous, especially woodcarving. While exploring the narrow streets of the town, you will find the workshops of craftsmen who still maintain the old traditions.

The northern half of the island (Meroi) is fertile and cultivated. The southern half, Vounó (mountain), is wilder with groves of holm oak. The semi-wild ponies of Skyros are said to be the horses depicted in the Parthenon frieze.

This ancient breed of pony can only be found on Skyros.

Information: There are good sandy beaches just to the north of Skyros Town. Try the local shellfish.
Port: Linariá
Size: 223km² (86sq miles)
Population: 3 000
How to get there: By air from Athens: daily flights in summer. By boat: ferries from mainland Greece.
Connections: To Skíathos.

SKÓPELOS

*busy tourist resorts – traditional architecture – fruit –
walking*

This fertile island
has long been
famous for its wine.
Evidence of Minoan
settlement has been
found including the
tomb of the
legendary King
Staphylos, credited
with first
introducing grapes
(*staphili*). The main
port, **Skópelos**, and
Glóssa in the north of the island, are two of
the most beautiful towns in the Sporades.
There are said to be 400 churches on

*There are a host of
places to pick up
souvenirs on
Skópelos.*

The Flying Dolphin
*hydrofoil
approaches the
beautiful town of
Glóssa.*

Skópelos and more than 120 in Skópelos Town alone. Exploring these, and occasionally discovering a beautiful icon or an interesting fresco, is a pleasant antidote to the tourist boutiques and souvenir shops which abound. For peace and quiet, there are two nunneries which can be visited: **Evangelístria**, with 14C icons, and **Timios Pródomos**, which involves a beautiful walk. Both are close to Skópelos Town, as is the monastery of Metamórphosis.

The wooded island of Dasia can be seen in the background of this panoramic view of Skópelos.

Information: Look for caique advertising trips to the island's beaches, including the famous Limnonári. Also look out for shoals of medusa jellyfish. The local dried plums and almonds are delicious.
Port: Skópelos (also Loutráki)
Size: 95km² (37sq miles)
Population: 4 500
How to get there: Ferries from mainland Greece.

Part of the coastline of the agriculturally rich island of Sámos.

EASTERN AND NORTHERN AEGEAN ISLANDS

The Greek islands which lie to the east of the Sporades and north of the Dodecanese do not really form an archipelago. Like all the Aegean islands, each is highly individual with a distinct character of its own. If the islands of this group have anything in common it is their close proximity to Asia Minor. They have always been in the firing line between

East and West – and they still are. Today there is a strong military presence on many of the islands. There is talk of oil deposits beneath the sea; Lemnos is strategically placed in the sea approaches to the Dardanelles and the Black Sea, just as it has always been. Once it was the Persians or the forces of Mithradates on the mainland, today it is Turkey. But the islands of the eastern and northern Aegean remain uncompromisingly and stubbornly Greek, despite everything history has thrown at them over the last 4 000 years.

ÁGIOS EFSTRÁTIOS

political exiles – oak trees – monk seals

Many of the visitors who have come to this remote place have not done so of their own free will: successive Greek governments have sent political prisoners here. Probably the most isolated island in the Aegean, it is named after the saint who died there in the 9C (even he was in exile). It is a place which does not expect tourists and is seldom disappointed. As a result there is very limited accommodation in the modern village which is far from picturesque. The deserted sandy beaches are difficult to reach except by caique .

Information: Bad weather can disrupt ferries
Port: Ágios Efstrátios
Size: 49km² (19sq miles)
Population: 250
How to get there: Ferry from Lemnos.

CHIOS (HÍOS)

Homer's birthplace – a terrible massacre – Mastic villages – a spectacular monastery – fine beaches

The traditional birthplace of Homer is a large island with strong mercantile traditions. From the earliest times until the

19C Chios was a major link in the sea trade between East and West. In antiquity, it was the first Greek city to deal in slaves; 2 000 years later in the 14C, Chios was still trading, by now a Genoese monopoly shipping Anatolian alum to the cloth makers of Bruges, as well as locally harvested mastic.

The Mastic villages (Mastikohória) in the south of the island, which were built at this time, are a must for every visitor. When the Chios mercantile fleet committed itself to the cause of Greek Independence and disrupted the supply of mastic, the Turkish reaction was swift and terrible. In 1822 30 000 Chiots were massacred, with many more enslaved or forcibly exiled. To this day, the north of the island has not really recovered. Nevertheless, there are places of interest to visit, for example, **Volissós** with its Homeric associations and long maritime tradition. Both here and nearby at **Limiá** are some of the best beaches on the island.

The excursion which every traveller should make is to **Néa Moní**, one of the most important and beautiful monuments in the Byzantine world. There are various buses and organized coach trips to the site. The earthquake of 1881, recent forest fires, and the impact of tourism have done nothing to detract from the beauty of the place.

All visitors should spend time exploring the old part of Chios Town. Find the **Citadel** (Kástro) and the **Small Palace** (Palatáki). There is also a wonderful bazaar south of the main square where bargain and souvenir hunters can spend many happy hours. The best place to be at the end of the day is in a taverna on the waterfront. Here the Chiots religiously observe the traditional evening promenade (*vólta*).

Information: Karfás is the nearest good beach to Chios Town, although there is much modern development.

Port: Chios

Size: 842km² (325sq miles)

Population: 49 000

How to get there: By air from Athens: 3 to 5 flights daily. By boat (ferry services): from Piraeus daily except Sundays (1 to 2 services); from Lesbos daily except Sundays; from Thessalonika weekly service via Lesbos.

Connections: 1 or 2 services weekly from Sámos and from Kavála once a week.

It is probable that man first learned to sail in the waters of the Aegean.

IKARÍA

hot springs – strong wine – fiercely independent islanders

When Icarus forgot the warning of his father, Daedalus, and flew too near the sun, they were passing over a windswept island which was to take his name. The sun's rays melted the wax which Daedalus had used to cement the feathers of the giant wings, and he saw his son plunge into the sea. It is now called the Icarian Sea, and the island is, of course, Ikaría.

According to another legend, the village of **Kámbos** south of the port is the site of ancient Inoi (*oenoe* means wine) where the vine was cultivated for the first time. It is a quiet little fishing village today with beautiful views. Visitors contemplating a pilgrimage will find robust wines made locally all over Ikaría.

Homemade wine is just one example of the islanders' legendary individualism and independence. They are friendly to visitors

A local fisherman sells some of his catch.

but do not especially wish to attract them to their rocky home. Traditionally, visitors came mainly for the hot springs at **Thérma**, reputed to cure arthritis, rheumatism and skin disorders. **Armenistís**, on the north coast, is a more attractive resort with excellent beaches.

Information: There are jeep safaris to the south of the island.
Port: Évdilos (and Thérma)
Size: 255km² (160sq miles)
Population: 7 600
How to get there: Ferry from Sámos.

LESBOS (LÉSVOS or MITLÍNI)
Sappho – bull sacrifice – a petrified forest – world-famous ouzo – minarets – glorious beaches – Picasso, Chagall and Matisse

This very large island, which the Turks called 'the garden of the empire' because it is so fertile, has something for everyone. But the distances between places – and the state of some roads – mean that trip-planning is

The rich soil of Lesbos provides farmers with an abundance of good crops, such as these lemons.

85

important. Lesbos is not as developed for tourism as many islands, but that gives it a special character. It is an island which will reward your efforts to get to know it better. Car hire is recommended, although there is a network of buses. Do not consider motor cycles: the distances are too great and the roads sometimes unpredictable.

The importance of Lesbos in antiquity can be judged by the great Hellenistic **amphitheatre** to the north of Mytilene, the port and capital. The Roman general Pompey had this splendid structure – with seats for 15 000 – copied in Rome. The past glories of Lesbos are displayed in the interesting **Archaeological Museum**. The town itself is well worth exploring before visiting the **Theophilos Museum** and adjacent **Teriade Museum**, with its fine collection of modern art, including works by Chagall, Picasso and Matisse, at Varia 4km (2½ miles) to the south.

Agiássos is a beautiful hill town in a green valley below Mt Olympus. Some of the best *ouzo* in Greece is made in the slightly ramshackle, charming coastal town of Plomári. But if you want a beach go on to **Vaterá** which has 7km (4 miles) of beautiful sand and a pleasant resort.

On the north of the island is the atmospheric town of **Míthimna** (Mólivos). Its great mansions and quiet, shuttered houses dream of past times and gaze across the sea to Turkey. The fountains and alleyways of Míthimna cast a spell on visitors and inhabitants alike. At Mandamádos, also in the north, is a less comforting relic of the past. Here, on the second Sunday after Easter a bull and other animals are sacrificed beneath a giant tree. There are similar echoes of the Mithras cult elsewhere on Lesbos.

Octopus left out to dry in the sun.

Visitors wishing to pay homage to Lesbos' most famous daughter – the poet Sappho – must travel to the eastern side of the island to **Ancient Eressós** and the pleasant beach resort of **Skála Eressoú**. The ruins of the ancient town where Sappho is said to have been born are on the hill to the east of the beach.

Returning to Mytilene at the end of your stay you might like to see the **Petrified Forest** near the Monastery of Ipsiloú. The huge fossilized stumps are thought to be 15 million years old.

Information: The fish is good, especially octopus in wine, sardines and the island's giant crayfish.
Port: Mytilene
Size: 1 630km² (630sq miles)
Population: 90 000
How to get there: By air: from Athens 4 to 5 services daily; from Thessalonika 1 to 2 services daily; from Lemnos 4 services a week; from Sámos and Chios 2 services a week; from Rhodes 2 services a week.

By ferry: from Piraeus 1 to 2 services daily;
from Chios 6 services a week; from Kavála 2
services a week.

LEMNOS (LÍMNOS)
*myths and legends – fine beaches – wine and seafood –
a Dardanelles memorial*

Visitors to Lemnos have an opportunity to
glimpse the history which underlies myth. We
know that at Polióhni on the east coast are the
remains of one of the oldest settlements in the
Aegean, dating from 4000 BC. The ability to
work metals – for war and agriculture – was an
important step in the development of
civilization. Appropriately enough, the island
is also the legendary home of Hephaistos, the
god of fire and metalwork.

Lemnos, lying in the approaches to the
Dardanelles, has always been strategic. In
1915 **Moúdros Bay** was the naval base from
which the British fleet launched the
Gallípoli assault. There was a military
hospital, and some of the 36 000 Allied dead
are buried nearby. In antiquity, Troy
controlled the straits and the Greeks
launched an assault. At Kavírio, across the
bay from Ifestía in the north of the island,
the legendary warrior Philoctetes lay in a
cave to recover from his wounds.

Archaeological evidence suggests that
there was widespread destruction of the
island's culture – either by war or
earthquake – in 2100 BC. Did this give rise to
the legend that Jason and the Argonauts
stayed several years on the island, long
enough to re-populate it?

The rich volcanic soils of Lemnos enable it
to produce an excellent dry, fruity wine. Food
sources flowing out of the Dardanelles from
the Black Sea mean that there is also plentiful

seafood, although occasionally poisonous
jellyfish are carried by the same currents.
There are many fine sandy beaches.

Information: Car or motorcycle hire is
recommended.
Port: Mírina
Size: 476km² (184sq miles)
Population: 16 000
How to get there: By air: from Athens 3 to 4
services daily; from Thessalonika 1 daily
service; from Lesbos 1 service daily.
By ferry: from Piraeus 2 services a week via
Chios and Lesbos; from Kavála 1 service a
week.
Connections: To Kími in Euboia and the
Sporades.

PSARÁ

a deserted monastery – an heroic history

It is a four-hour trip over difficult seas to this
barren historic island which has bred many
generations of tough sailors. The hero of
Greek Independence, Admiral Kanaris, is its

*Fishing is a vital
part of the islands'
economy.*

most famous son. In his day it was the home port of Greece's third largest merchant fleet. But after his attack on the Turkish fleet the island was made to pay. A few escaped to French ships, but most of the sizeable population retreated to a powder magazine pursued by Turkish forces. Here on the 'black ridge of Psará, they detonated the powder.

A view of the tree-clad hills of Sámos over a church.

Information: Accommodation is limited. There are some good beaches.
Size: 40km² (15.4sq miles)
Population: 450
How to get there: Ferry three times a week from Chios.

SÁMOS

pine trees and nightingales – excellent beaches – villas – a wonder of the ancient world – rich history

The green island of Sámos – once the richest in the Aegean – has always prized excellence. The legendary birthplace of Hera, queen of the gods, also nurtured the mathematician Pythagoras, the philosopher Epicurus, and the astronomer Aristarchos, who first discovered that the earth revolves around the sun. Under the brilliant tyrant Polycrates, the fleet of five-tiered *samaines* dominated trade in the Aegean.

Visitors can glimpse something of the wealth and exotic influences which characterized ancient Sámos by visiting the **Archaeological Museum** in Sámos Town (Vathí). Beneath the magnificent Greek koúros are figures of the Egyptian gods Osiris and Horus; there are also ivories, bronzes and other riches from Mesopotamia and further east. The Persians crucified Polycrates in 522 BC, acquiring the island and all its riches.

The most remarkable of Polycrates' achievements can be seen in the port of

Pithagório. The great subterranean aqueduct which brought fresh water to his capital was one of the wonders of the ancient world. This and many other sites (including the ancient wall and Roman baths) add interest to a large, unashamed holiday resort.

Tourist development has marched quietly but remorselessly along the north-east. The

The picturesque harbour of Karlovássi on Sámos.

popular resort of Kokári is still pretty, with windsurfers among the few remaining fishermen. But inland from this part of the coast is a landscape where Pan himself would be happy to roam: valleys of chestnut and plane, alive with running water and birdsong; vineyards and dark cypresses reaching into a lapis lazuli sky. Visit **Vourliótes** and the **Vrondianí** monastery. Or drive up the Aidónia Gorge (Nightingale Gorge) to Manolátes.

Sámos's best beaches are in the north-west (beyond the commercial port of Karlovássi) at **Potámi**, or in the south-west at **Psilí Ámos** (fine sand).

Information: Forest fires can start very easily in Sámos – take special care.
Ports: Vathí and Pithagório (east); Karlovássi (west)
Size: 477km² (184sq miles)
Population 32 000
How to get there: By air: from Athens 4 to 5 services daily. By ferry: daily services from Piraeus.
Connections: Boats to Turkish coast in season.

SAMOTHRACE (SAMOTHRÁKI)

a sacred island – the Sanctuary of the Great Gods – an imposing mountain – woods and thermal springs

This is the spiritual centre of the North Aegean. From the Bronze Age until the fall of Rome, great kings and ordinary people made the pilgrimage to Samothrace to be initiated into the Mysteries and to sacrifice to the Great Gods. We know that Phillip of Macedon, father of Alexander the Great, made the pilgrimage; Ptolemy, king of Egypt, added an imposing gateway to the shrine. Just what the Mysteries involved we may never know: to write of them was forbidden and would incur the wrath of the Sanctuary's fearsome protective demons, the *kábeiroi*. The principal deity seems to have been the Great Mother, with a subordinate male consort.

The approach to Samothrace is the most impressive in the Aegean after Santoríni, but as access is from the mainland surprisingly few make the journey. The famous 'winged victory' is now in the Louvre, but the **Museum** is full of interesting art and relics. The **Ruins of the Sanctuary** themselves are awesome.

Information: The best guide to Samothrace is by Karl Lehmann who excavated the site. There is accommodation, a bus service around the island and some good beaches.

Port: Kamariótissa

Size: 178km² (69sq miles)

Population 2 900

How to get there: By air: from Athens to Alexandroúpoli (1 to 2 services daily) and continuing by boat. By ferry: from Alexandroúpoli, daily service, from Kavála, 3 services a week in summer.

THÁSSOS

forests of pine, chestnut, oak and cypress – a shrine to Pan – sandy beaches – holiday resorts

The island has always been popular with Greek holidaymakers but tourism co-exists with the traditional economy based on agriculture and quarrying, which means that this verdant island retains its own special character – and charm.

Thássos Town, also known as **Liménas**, has a good natural harbour. The island's abundant oil, wine, marble – and especially gold – made this an important place in antiquity. The ruins are well worth exploring. Climb up the **ramparts** from the harbour to

the magnificent theatre (converted for animal fights by the Romans!) Higher up is the **acropolis** with temples to Apollo, Athena and a sanctuary to Pan.

Donkeys still share an important amount of work on Greek farms.

A good coast road circles the island. The best beaches are in the south, look out for **Alikí** and **Astrída**. **Limenária** is a pleasant holiday resort.

Information: Mosquitoes can be a problem. The local red wine is excellent, as is the honey and walnut preserve.
Port: Thássos
Size: 379km² (147sq miles)
Population: 13 200
How to get there: By air: from Kavála, continuing by boat. By ferry: from Kavála to Thássos Town (Liménas) daily.

ISLANDS OF THE SARONIC GULF

Despite their proximity to Athens and the influence this has exerted upon them, the islands of the Saronic Gulf have retained strong identities of their own. Each island is completely different from the others, and each benefits from being explored out of season, if possible. In spring, or at the very end of summer, the spirit of each place is less elusive, less likely to be lost in the hubub of fellow visitors or Athenian weekenders.

AEGINA (ÉGINA)

a great temple – pistachio nuts – tourist hotels – earthenware pots

Visitors can, of course, treat Aegina as many Athenians do – as the best swimming close to the city. **Kolóna** is the best sandy beach near Aegina Town, or there is **Marathónas** further south. On the far (eastern) side of the island is the package holiday resort of **Agía Marína**.

The holiday resort of Agiá Marína has some of the best swimming facilities on the island.

A feature of Aegina Town is the wide range of fruit for sale from boats in the harbour.

The best swimming and cleanest water involves a caique trip from Pérdika to the islet of **Moní**, uninhabited but for wild goats and a campsite.

There is another Aegina. The working port itself is interesting. Here are the historic houses of Greece's first prime minister, and great naval heros, such as Kanaris. In the Livádia suburbs is the house where Kazantzakis wrote *Zorba the Greek*. But on the other side of Aegina is something no visitor should miss: the **Temple of Aphaia**. This glorious Doric building is a reminder of Aegina's golden age, when the island struck its own coinage and its fleet rivalled that of

This stone church overlooks the harbour in Aegina Town.

Athens. But as King Minos wanted the maiden Aphaia, so Athens wanted Aegina; and in the 5C BC it took it.

The Doric-style ruins of the Temple of Aphaia on Aegina.

Information: The island's pistachio orchards are famous, as are its earthenware pots. In the days before refrigeration, Aegina jugs and pitchers were used to keep water cool throughout Greece. Today, they are mostly used as ornaments.

Port: Aegina (Égina)

Size: 83km² (32sq miles)

Population: 11 500

How to get there: Ferries and hydrofoil from Piraeus. Day cruises from Piraeus.

ANGÍSTRI

pines – farmers and fishermen – modern tourism

This fertile little island supports a traditional community which goes about its age-old tasks, oblivious to the modern development at Skála that has developed in the north of the island. The other settlement, Milos, has a little more character, but it is Angístri's pine-covered interior and the beaches of **Drakonéra** and **Limenária** which are the secret of its quiet appeal.

Information: Mountain bikes can be hired, or motorcycles for the less energetic.
Port: Skála
Size: 12km² (4.6sq miles)
Population: 700
How to get there: Ferry from Piraeus.

HYDRA (ÍDRA)

impressive stone mansions – a beautiful harbour – discos – donkeys – fireboats

'What would you do in my place?' Lord Nelson asked Andreas Miaoúlis whom he caught breaking the British blockade off Toulon with a ship full of wheat. 'Hang you' replied Miaoúlis. Nelson was delighted, and let him go. Like many of those who made vast fortunes supplying France with Black Sea grain and built the fine mansions of Hydra, Miaoúlis and his fleet fought heroically in the Greek War of Independence. In June each year Hydra celebrates the famous fire-ship attack of the then Admiral Miaoúlis, with a festival ending in the burning of a ship at sea. Finding accommodation in Hydra during the festival is difficult, but so it is throughout the summer in the beautiful and deservedly popular town.

Across the rooftops of Hydra.

It is an island of extremes. The town is crowded, cosmopolitan and rather expensive, with a busy nightlife. The interior has no tarmac, no motorized vehicles and relies on donkeys for transport. The beaches are mainly rocky: the cleanest are more easily accessible by boat.

Information: Windsurfing is popular on Hydra. Try the almond cakes (*amigdalotá*).
Port: Hydra (Ídra)
Size: 50km² (19sq miles)
Population: 3 000
How to get there: By boat from Piraeus: regular services in about 4 hours; express service 2½ hours. By hydrofoil from Piraeus.
Connections: Hydrofoil to east coast of Peloponnese.

PÓROS

a pleasant town – the Temple of Poseidon –
Demosthenes – views of Argolis

Póros means 'a ford', and the island (just) is a
convenient stepping stone or base from which
to explore the mainland. Short excursions
from Póros via the ferry will bring you to the
ruins of **Mycenae** 'rich in gold'; **Tiryns** 'of the
mighty walls' and the incomparable theatre at
Epidauros. Much nearer is delightful
Lemonodássos, a vast lemon grove bearing
fruit and flowers all year round.

   On Póros itself take time to visit the few
remaining pillars of the great **Temple of
Poseidon** (Naós Possidóna). Here, in
October 322 BC, Athens' greatest statesman
Demosthenes committed suicide, cheating
the Thracian execution squad which had
pursued him. Having sucked poison from
his pen while pretending to write a last
letter, Demosthenes quit his sanctuary: 'I, O
gracious Poseidon, quit thy temple while I
yet live; Antipater and his Macedonians have
done what they could to pollute it.'

Information: The best beach is **Kanáli**. There is
   plenty of accommodation and some good
   tavernas.
Port: Póros
Size: 23km² (9sq miles)
Population: 4 000
How to get there: Regular ferries from Piraeus;
   also hydrofoil. Day cruises from Piraeus. Car
   ferry from Galatás.

SALAMIS (SALAMÍNA)

Only those tired of life would go to Salamis
to swim, but there is nowhere better to sit in
a taverna – perhaps in the pleasant little
resorts of Selínia or Eádio – and reflect on

Greece's unique maritime tradition. It was at Salamis, of course, in 480 BC that the greatly outnumbered Athenian ships destroyed the Persian fleet. It could be argued that Salamis was one of the most important battles in history: drawing a line between East and West. Nearly 2 500 years later Salamis is still the major Greek naval base. Across the water, at night, you can see the lights of Piraeus where Greek ship-owners like to moor their private yachts. The Greek mercantile fleet sails the oceans of the world and the wealth and power of the ship-owning families is legendary. If, as many archaeologists believe, man first learned to sail island-hopping in the Aegean, it may explain Greece's unique relationship with the sea.

At dawn with the ferries at Piraeus.

Information: The authorities are now dealing with the problem of sea pollution near to Athens.
Port: Paloúkia
Size: 96km² (37sq miles)
Population: 29 000
How to get there: By ferry from Piraeus and Pérama.

SPETSAI (SPÉTSES)

ship-owners – superb beaches and watersports – pine trees – The Magus *– horse-drawn cabs*

This strange, eccentric island is very popular with Athenians. There are no private cars on Spetsai; both visitors and residents must use buses, boats or horse-drawn vehicles. In the Greek War of Independence, the ships of Spetsai (together with those of Psára and Hydra) played a vital role. The splendid mansion of the island's leader – Hatzigianni-Mexi – is now a museum. Look for relics of the heroic woman admiral, Laskarina-Bouboulina.

While leaving the town heading west for a circuit of the island, you will see the empty buildings of Anágiros College. The novelist John Fowles was a teacher here and used the school and many other features of the island in *The Magus*. The first of many fine beaches is **Vrelloú**, and further on is scenic **Zogeriá**. Round to the south are Agía Paraskeví cove, and beyond that the finest beach in the Saronic islands, **Agía Anárgiri**. The interesting looking islet to the east of Spetsai, Spetsopoúla, is privately owned (by the legendary shipping tycoon Stávros Niárchos).

Information: Food on Spetsai is generally of a very high standard. Try fish '*a la Spetsiosa*': baked in the oven with olive oil, tomato, garlic and bay leaf.

Port: Spétses (Spetsai)

Size: 22km² (9sq miles)

Population: 3 800

How to get there: By ferry: daily service from Piraeus. By hydrofoil from Piraeus (Zéa): many services daily.

ENJOYING YOUR VISIT

SWIMMING AND WATERSPORTS

An island holiday in the Aegean offers
infinite possibilities for enjoying yourself in
and on the water. But Poseidon, the sea god,
was not known for his even temper. Aegean
squalls are notorious. The whole nature of
the sea can change suddenly when the
meltémi blows and lifeguards are very rare:
you are much more likely to be *on your own*.
Do not swim out very far, that tempting rock
or islet is always further away than you think.
Around many of the islands there are
ferocious currents and undertows; even
the strongest swimmer should take special
care.

See A-Z for Windsurfing, Waterskiing,
Scuba Diving and Boats and Sailing.

FOOD AND DRINK

When to Eat

Greeks have lunch between 2 and 3pm and
dinner from 9pm to around 11pm. For
breakfast find a patisserie on the larger
islands, or somewhere that serves set
yoghurt covered with honey tasting of the
flowers and trees of the island. On the
smallest island you should find a coffee shop
(*kafenío*). Greek coffee is 'cooked' and
served with the grounds in the cup (it
should be sipped rather than drunk).
(Skétos – no sugar; Métrios – medium sweet;
Glikós – very sweet.) Alternatively ask for
kafes frappé: delicious iced coffee. The *kafenío*
is the place to have the classic aperitif, *ouzo*,
at around 6 or 7pm to watch the world go by.
Add a little water or ice to the aniseed spirit.
Traditionally a few *mezédes* – olives; nuts;
octopus – would be served automatically
(and free) with *ouzo* but this is rare now.

Restaurants come in all shapes and sizes on the Greek islands. This one has superb views across Alónissos.

Where to Eat

There are specialist establishments (game, offal) and more elaborate restaurants (*estiatória*) but generally Greeks eat in tavernas. These range from basic to smart but the least pretentious often serve the best food. A hut by the roadside may have the best *souvláki* (kebab) you ever tasted (as the first king of Greece discovered when his chef repeatedly failed to reproduce the experience in the royal kitchen). Picnics are fun in the islands, with good bread, fruit, olives and *féta* (the salty, pungent sheep's cheese).

ENJOYING YOUR VISIT

What to Eat

Pre-prepared dishes are often warm rather than hot, which is the way Greeks prefer it. It is possible – if they are good and varied – to make an entire meal out of *mezédes* (hors d'oeuvres). Or to try a few, followed by a main dish (a roast or casserole) or *tís óras*: fish and meat cooked to order.

One of the sweetest smelling places in a Greek village is its bakery.

Fish – The waiter should always ask you to go and choose your fish. If he does not, insist. No Greek would eat a fish unseen, it is a national ritual. And keep an eye on the fish you have chosen: some crafty taverna owners will weigh your fish in front of you and then cook you another cheaper one. A sea bream (*tsipoúra*) can sometimes be changed for a (*sargós*) – tasty but not the same and bought for half the price. This is all part of the good-natured drama (sometimes comedy, sometimes tragedy) of a Greek meal.

Wine – Wherever possible in the islands drink local wine, preferably *híma* (from the barrel). Most wines are white, many have pine resin added (*retsína*) which in antiquity was to preserve the wine but has become a Greek passion. It is no more artificial than the oak so valued in the wines from other countries: persevere, it is part of the Greek experience. The volcanic islands produce the best wines. There are also some interesting reds to be found.

Some Island Specialities

Ándros – *kolokitholoúlouda tiganitá*: the flower of the marrow fried in batter.

Mykonos – *kremidópita*: finely chopped onions, mixed with soft cheese, spread over layers of pastry and baked in an oven.

Náxos – *katsíki* or *arní patoúdo*: lamb or kid stuffed with liver, rice and hard cheese (*kefalotíra*) and baked in the oven.

Páros – *saligária psitá*: baked snails.

Santoríni – *psefdokeftédes* 'pseudo-keftedes': dough balls flavoured with tomato, mint and cinnamon, and fried.

Tenos – *patatoú*: mashed potatoes mixed with cheese, eggs, toasted crumbs and parsley, spiced with nutmeg and pepper and baked in the oven.

THE BASICS

Before You Go

No inoculations are required before visiting Greece, but you are advised to have a typhoid/cholera booster, and to check that you are covered against tetanus and polio.

Only a valid passport is required for entry into Greece.

Getting There

By air Most flights to Greece and the Greek Islands from North America and Australia either land at Athens or at another European city from which passengers are then transferred.

You can fly directly from many UK airports to several Greek Islands such as Rhodes, Kos, Páros, Mykonos, Skíathos and Santoríni, and get connecting flights from Athens to many more. Flights are either scheduled or chartered, and the latter offer a host of holiday opportunities at highly competitive rates.

By ferry For the smaller and more remote islands you will have to travel by ferry, either directly from Piraeus, Rhodes or Crete, or via other islands; with a package deal this is all included in the price, and couriers will smooth your path through all the different ports

and airports. You can get timetables from the tourist offices, but do not depend too heavily on their accuracy.

Tickets are bought from the shipping line offices or at mobile counters on the dockside, and it may be necessary to book in advance for berths on night ferries, for the hydrofoil, for car ferries, and for everything in the height of the season.

By rail It is possible to travel from various major cities in Europe to Greece. With former Yugoslavia now inaccessible to tourists, the routes from the west are limited. The railway is

Car ferries, such as this to Antíparos, may be the only way you can visit the more secluded of the islands.

an expensive means of travel unless you use an InterRail pass. Anyone living in Europe for at least six months is eligible for one, and they are available from British Rail or any travel agent. Eurail passes are the equivalent which can be bought by Australians and North Americans before they arrive in Europe.

By coach   These are probably the cheapest means of travelling to Greece, and from Britain the journey takes from three to four days depending on stopovers. Beware of some disreputable companies which do not comply with the regulations.

By car   Driving across Europe can be enjoyable if you are not short of time, but with former Yugoslavia a no-go area, the main route open is through France and Italy to the Adriatic ferries. Crossings from Italy leave from Ancona, Bari, Brindisi, Ortona, Otranto, Venice or Trieste; some of these run several crossings every day throughout the year, while others operate in high season only. Distances covered and thus prices vary greatly. *See also* **Tourist Information Offices** and **Transport**.

Arriving

The duty and tax-free allowances on goods depend on whether they were bought duty free or outside the EU, or purchased with duty paid within the EU. Get a copy of HM Customs and Excise regulations at any airport or local customs office to check.

There are three terminals at Athens airport: one deals solely with Olympic Airways, one with charter flights and the other handles the remaining international flights. From either of these you can get a bus to Piraeus if you are travelling on independently to one or more of the islands by ferry. Express bus no 19 runs every half hour (and also between the terminals).

Those on package holidays will be met by a representative of their holiday company and will be helped with their connections. If you need assistance on making onward bookings, contact the Greek National Tourist Office (GNTO/EOT) at the airport.

Several islands have their own airports, and these are usually tiny affairs which you get through in a very short time. Again, those on package tours or holidays will be met by a travel representative and whisked off in a coach. Anyone arriving on their own can usually get a bus or a taxi to their destination.

A-Z

Accidents and Breakdowns

Fully comprehensive insurance is advisable, and motoring organizations recommend that you carry a green card although this is no longer a legal requirement. Check with your insurance company before leaving home for what you should do in case of an accident. You should carry with you a fire extinguisher, first-aid kit, and a breakdown warning triangle.

If you have hired a car, insist that you have a collision waiver and that you are fully insured for road accidents. Should you be involved in an accident it is illegal to drive away from the scene. Choose an international car hire agency over a small local one where possible even if it costs more, and you will be guaranteed a well-serviced car plus breakdown assistance if you should be stranded. Mopeds can be dangerous to drive, and many tour operators advise against hiring them. Motoring organizations are not represented on most islands.

Accommodation

Places to stay vary widely, and while some islands and towns boast smart hotels, in others the best room you will be able to get will be in someone's house. The rule is to book ahead if you want to stay in a hotel, especially in the height of the summer when demand exceeds supply.

If you are prepared to be more flexible, you can simply arrive off the ferry and wait to be offered a room by a private landlord. Check with the local tourist office to see what they recommend if you want to play safe, but you should find that the accommodation is clean and will suit your needs for a night or two. These rooms are officially controlled and graded, and facilities usually include a toilet and shower, even if they are shared with the family. In the winter they are closed in order to keep the hotels in business.

The GNTO (EOT) also lets traditional lodgings in some out-of-the-way places, usually in renovated buildings in typical settings, and you can get details of these from local tourist offices. Villas for rent are very popular with holiday-makers, and if you don't want to book one with a package tour operator, you can often find one when you get there. Ask around to see if anyone knows of a villa to rent.

Youth hostels are pretty well unheard of in the Aegean Islands, but accommodation is often so cheap that most young travellers can afford it (*see also* **Camping**).

Airports see **Arriving p.109**

Babysitters see **Children**

Banks
Greek banks usually open 0830–1530, Monday to Friday. In the major cities and tourist areas certain branches are also open for part of the evening and on Saturday mornings. Commission rates vary from bank to bank, so ask before entering into a transaction.

Beaches
These are what a holiday in the Greek Islands is all about, and there are plenty of idyllic

Clean, hygienic beaches, such as this at Kamári on Santoríni, make spending your time on the shore a delight.

beaches that are perfectly safe for children. On some islands it may take a boat ride to get to the best beaches, and it is usually worth the extra effort. Tavernas are often strategically placed just off the beach, offering food and drink throughout the long, hot day.

Remember that nude swimming or sunbathing is almost certainly illegal, although the authorities might turn a blind eye where it is discreetly carried out.

Bicycles

Bicycles are often available to hire from the larger holiday resorts, and sometimes from less frequented places as well. They are not expensive to rent, and you may be able to get a reduction for a longer period of rental. Bikes can be carried free on ferries, and in the guard's van on trains for a small fee; you might also be able to strap a cycle on the back or the roof of buses.

Breakdowns see Accidents

Buses see Transport

Camping

Camping is illegal outside official camping sites, and the police can enforce the law if they discover anyone doing this. Unofficially, as long as you are not sleeping rough on the beach, or fouling any public areas, the police turn a blind eye; do make sure to ask the permission locally before pitching camp, from the village taverna or café.

Official sites vary from place to place, and the facilities they offer range from very basic to highly organized. There are also private campsites which are very cheap.

Car Hire

Car hire is very expensive in Greece but remains the best way to see some of the islands. The major international hire companies have offices in tourist towns and in the islands, and some medium-sized firms which also have several branches are quite reputable and considerably cheaper.

Watch out for the cut-price local firm which may seem to offer a bargain but whose vehicles might not be so rigorously serviced or in a roadworthy condition. If you do choose a small agency, make sure that the proper insurance cover is provided and insist on having collision damage waiver, even if this adds to the costs.

To hire a car you need to be at least 21 and sometimes 25,

It is perhaps not the safest way to get around, but a moped can allow you to visit some of the less accessible sites.

and have a full driver's licence if you are an EU national, or an international driver's licence if you are not. Payment is usually by credit card; if you do not have one a large cash deposit will be required.

Check the brakes and tyres before you take the car, and fill up with petrol when you can as petrol stations are scarce in country regions. Mopeds can be very dangerous to drive on rough island roads. *See also* **Accidents and Breakdowns.**

Children

Small people are loved and valued by the Greeks, and they like to keep them by their side until very late at night. Your children will be as welcome in tavernas and restaurants as on the beach, and nobody will give them disapproving looks if they are lively, except other northern Europeans. The Greek Islands were made for young children, with their safe, sandy beaches and warm, clear and very clean seas. Remember how hot the sun is, even if the day is cloudy or the wind blowing, and keep children – and yourself – well covered with sun creams and hats. The midday sun is especially fierce. Disposable nappies and baby foods are fairly easy to find in the more popular resorts, but particular brands of baby milk and food are scarce or impossible to get hold of in remote regions. If in doubt, bring your own.

Babysitting is probably easier to organize in private villas, apartments and pensions than in hotels.

Churches see **Religion**

Climate see **p.15**

A traditional Greek Orthodox Church on the island of Santoríni.

Clothing

At the time of year when the vast majority of tourists go to the Greek Islands, the weather is extremely hot, and the minimum of clothes will be needed. Bear in mind, though, that the evenings can be cool, and when the winds blow for several days at a time it can also be chilly. Cover up in the midday sun, too, and remember to wear a hat. Respect the feelings of the native Greeks when you wander into shops, banks and restaurants, and wear something over a bikini or shorts.

Nudity is illegal on many beaches even if it is tolerated on many more, and topless bathing or sunbathing is often frowned on but accepted. The police are unlikely to swoop onto a beach and arrest everyone without their clothes on, but just bear in mind that they can do it if they wish, and try to remain sensitive to traditional local feelings. *See also* **Etiquette**.

Complaints

Try to make any complaints in a calm, unhurried manner, at the time, and to the correct person. If in doubt, ask the Tourist Police for help and advice, or enlist the support of the local tourist office.

Consulates and Embassies

They can be found at the following addresses:

British Embassy:
1 Odos Ploutarkhou,
Athens 10675
☎ 906 75-723 6211.

British Consulate:
24 Akti Possidonis, Piraeus
☎ 01-4178345.

American Embassy:
91 Vasilissis Sofias Avenue,
Athens
☎ 115 21-7212951.

Canadian Embassy:
4 Ioannou Genadiou Street,
Athens
☎ 115 21-7239511.

Australian Embassy:
37D, Soutsou Street, Athens
☎ 115 21-6647303.

New Zealand Embassy:
15 An. Tsoha Street, Athens
☎ 115 21-6410311.
In an emergency, contact the Tourist Police on the individual island.

Crime

The Greek Islands are mainly crime-free, apart from that brought in by holidaymakers. Drugs are absolutely illegal, and anyone caught using or dealing in drugs will be harshly punished. The police can also make arrests for nude bathing and sunbathing, and for drunk and disorderly behaviour. Greeks themselves are usually scrupulously honest, but the many other nationals who either live in or visit Greece are often not, so take as much care of your belongings as you would in any other European country.

Currency *see* **Money**

Customs and Entry Regulations *see* **Arriving p.109**

Disabled Visitors

The National Tourist Organisation of Greece (EOT) publishes a questionnaire which you can send ahead to hotels or owners of villas or apartments to check out your requirements. Remember that much of the attraction of the Greek Islands lies in its rocky terrain, essential journeys in small boats, and small, winding and hilly streets.

RADAR, at 25 Mortimer Street, London W1N 8AB; ☎ 0171 637 5400, publish fact sheets, as well as an annual guide to facilities and accommodation overseas.

Driving

Nationals of EU countries only need a full driving licence, but an international driving licence is required by those from other countries. Fully comprehensive insurance is advisable, and motoring organizations recommend that you carry a green card although this is no longer a legal requirement. Check with your insurance company before leaving home for what you should do in case of an accident.

You need to carry a fire extinguisher, first-aid kit, and breakdown warning triangle. Petrol is often hard to come by in the evenings and at weekends, so be sure to keep your tank full if you will need to drive at those times, and especially if you go into remote mountainous districts.

The motoring organizations are represented only on the larger islands, but most small towns have a mechanic who will come to your aid in the case of a breakdown.

Speed limits in built-up areas are 50kph (31mph), and 80kph (50mph) outside built-up areas. Undipped headlights must not be used in towns, only sidelights.

Dry Cleaning see Laundry

Electric Current

The usual current is 220 volts, and electric plugs have large round pins. An adaptor is essential.

Embassies see Consulates

Emergencies see Police and Consulates

Etiquette

Care should be taken to cover up decently when going to monasteries, churches and some of the ancient sites – this applies as much to men as to women. Shorts and bare shoulders are frowned upon, as are women in mini-skirts and trousers.

The Greeks consider it an insult if a hand is held up to them with the palm pointing outwards, as if to indicate the number five. They often express 'No' by looking up and

The Greeks have a calm and collected outlook on life.

nodding their head upwards – do not confuse this with 'Yes'!

Remember that the Greeks take a siesta in the afternoon, an antidote to the early mornings and late nights they keep in the summer months. Respect this by not making too much noise between 2 and 5pm. Also respect the Greeks by not being in a hurry, and never trying to rush them. Meals are meant to be leisurely, so if fast food is your idea of pleasure, don't go to Greece!

Excursions

Evidence of classical Greece is everywhere, and during your stay you will probably want to visit at least one temple, monastery or archaeological site. You can book tours and excursions as part of your package holiday, or find

Pleasure boats mingle with the local fishing boats.

details of them chalked up on a blackboard in the harbour to be picked at random depending on what day you want to travel.

Some boat trips include snorkelling on suitable beaches, or anchoring in a beautiful bay to barbecue or picnic, swim and sunbathe. *See also* **Tourist Information Offices.**

Guidebooks *see* Maps

Health

EU nationals should carry a Form E111 (forms available from post offices) which entitles the holder to free urgent treatment for accident or illness in EU countries. The treatment will have to be paid for in the first instance, but can be reclaimed later. EU and non-EU nationals are advised to take out comprehensive insurance cover, and to keep bills, receipts and invoices to support any claim.

Lists of doctors can be obtained from hotels, chemists or the tourist police, and first aid and medical advice is also available at pharmacies (*farmakio*); Greek pharmacists are very highly qualified. The latter are generally open from 9am–1pm, and 5–7pm, and those which are open late or on Sundays display notices on their doors.

Sunstroke causes much misery on holiday, and you are advised to wear a hat, not allow yourself to get burnt, and drink plenty of fluids. Watch out, too, for the ubiquitous mosquito, and use a repellent if you are a particular target.

Hours *see* Opening Hours

Information *see* Tourist Information Offices

Language

The Greek alphabet is completely individual with many letters that translate the same as the Roman alphabet but also several unfamiliar ones. To read signs and destinations it would be wise to learn the letters, a relatively simple task. Many Greeks speak some English, and the younger ones especially enjoy practising their skills with English speakers. On the busiest and most popular islands it should be an easy matter to make yourself understood, and even on smaller, more remote islands a little English is often known. The few words and phrases shown opposite should get you started on learning what is a very beautiful language.

Laundry

Launderettes are increasingly to be found, especially in the

Yes/no	né/óhi
good morning	kaliméra
good evening	kalispéra
please/thank you	parakaló/ evkaristó
where?/when?	pou?/póte?
today/tomorrow	símera/ávrio
sorry	signómi
How much is it?	pósso káni aftó?

Greek can be an extremely difficult language to grasp. It is lucky that many islanders speak English to some degree.

larger resorts and towns; sometimes you can get a service wash done for a little extra. Otherwise ask the owner of your accommodation where you can wash your clothes, and thanks to the climate they will usually be dry very soon after being hung out.

Lost Property

Lost or stolen travellers' cheques and credit cards should be reported immediately to the issuing company along with a list of numbers, and the police should also be informed. If anything else goes missing, report it to the police and get a report from them for insurance purposes. Unless the property is very valuable they will probably not be very interested, and this will certainly apply to credit cards and travellers' cheques.

Maps and Guides

You need to take locally bought maps with a pinch of salt, especially those covering fairly remote areas. If you need very accurate information, take with you a copy of the Michelin map 980 which covers Greece. The *Michelin Green Guide Greece* also has many maps and more information on the popular islands. Maps of individual islands are easy to come by *in situ*, but they are often completely inaccurate and terribly confusing. Often what turns out to be a mere track will be marked as a road, and roads which are still in the planning stage are marked as built.

Medical Care *see* Health

Money

The Greek unit of currency is the drachma, and notes in circulation include those of 100, 500, 1 000, 5 000 and 10 000; coins come in denominations of 5, 10, 20, 50 and 100. Check with your bank to see how much Greek currency can be imported and exported. Bring travellers' cheques rather than hard cash into the islands for safety reasons, but be prepared to have a limited number of outlets at which to change them, and consequently not necessarily the best rate of exchange.

Foreign currency, travellers' cheques and Eurocheques can be exchanged at airport arrival lounges, and at the banks, post offices and exchange kiosks in larger towns and resorts. Hotels will also cash travellers' cheques, and there are often

automatic cash dispensers. Post offices are ideal places to take your travellers' cheques, since even those small islands without a bank or exchange bureau usually have one.

Credit cards tend to be accepted only at larger hotels and more expensive restaurants, although they are essential if you want to hire a car. You can get cash advances on credit cards from a bank, but will probably have to cash a large sum.

Newspapers

Foreign language newspapers and magazines are on sale in the main tourist centres and in large towns, but they are usually a day or two out of date. The daily English-language *Athens News* and the Greek *Weekly News* are also on sale in these places, and in Rhodes there is a small weekly paper produced by the local English community.

Opening Hours

Banks: usually 8.30am–3.30pm, with some variations.
Shops: 8.30am–4.30pm, Monday and Wednesday; 8.30am–2pm, and 5–8pm, Tuesday, Thursday and Friday; 8.30am–3.30pm, Saturday. Some shops may close in mid-afternoon during the summer, but tourist shops usually stay

open very late in the evening.
Chemists: open as for shops,
but usually closed in the
evenings and at weekends.
There should be a sign on the
door referring you to the
nearest late opening one.
Monasteries – for which there
are no visiting hours as such –
are generally closed between 1
and 5pm.

Photography

The Greek Islands are a photo-
grapher's dream, with every
new turning bringing with it the
perfect view, and the natural
light usually bright. Remember
to adjust your camera and/or
film accordingly.

Film is usually widely
available if expensive and in
limited form, but bring any
spares with you as they may be
hard to come by; batteries for
automatic cameras, for
example, are difficult to find.

Cameras are banned in some
museums, and where they are
allowed you may need to buy a
special ticket; it is unlikely that
flashes are permitted.

Police

Greek Tourist Police are quite
approachable and friendly to
visitors, and can often help
with finding accommodation
and providing information. *See
also* **Crime** and **Camping**

*Colourful flowers, such as these
on a house in Náxos, are a
feature of many villages.*

Post Offices

Post offices and post boxes are
painted bright yellow, and sell
stamps, although these can
also be bought at kiosks. Post
offices in larger towns and
resorts tend to be open all day
Monday to Friday, and on
Saturday mornings, but in
other places they may close at
lunchtime and open again
during odd hours in the
evening. The postal service,
especially from the islands, is

slow, and postcards will arrive home long after you have.

Public Holidays

New Year's Day: 1 January
Epiphany: 6 January
First Monday in Lent
Independence Day: 25 March
Good Friday, Easter Sunday and Monday (Orthodox calendar)
Labour Day: 1 May
Whit Sunday and Monday (Orthodox calendar)
Assumption: 15 August

A Greek Easter meal including bread and dyed eggs.

Ochi (No) Day: 28 October
Christmas Day and Boxing Day: 25 and 26 December.

Every island also has a holiday on its Saint's Day and on annual festival days. On these days, and also the above, all shops and businesses close on the afternoon before and the morning after, as well as on the Monday if the holiday falls on a Sunday.

Public Transport *see* Transport

Religion

Virtually all of the population belongs to the Greek Orthodox

Church, with a small number of Catholics, Jews and Muslims in little pockets throughout the country. Don't expect to find your church represented on the islands, however.

Stamps *see* **Post Offices**

Taxis *see* **Transport**

Telephones
The telephone service (OTE) is separate from the post office, and office opening hours vary from place to place. OTE offices are the best place from which to make an overseas phone call, and the only place you are able to reverse the charges, but you should be prepared for a long wait even if you are making an operator-assisted call.

In very large towns there is often an OTE office open 24 hours, but in smaller places the office hours are very restricted. Dial 161 for the international operator, or to ring a foreign number direct, dial 00 followed by the country code (44 for the UK, 1 for the USA and Canada, 61 for Australia), then the city or district code and the number.

Local calls may be made from red pay phones in hotels or restaurants, and all kinds of calls from phone kiosks in the street where you pay after you have made the call. Making international calls from these kiosks is very difficult, and the lines are often poor. Calls from hotels are extremely expensive. Cheap rates only for calls made within Greece apply from 3–5pm, and 9pm–8am plus all weekend, and there is a small reduction in the cost of international calls made after 10pm, but only from the mainland.

Time Difference
Greek time is GMT plus 2 hours all year round.

Tipping
Prices are usually inclusive of service, including taxis, but it is considered polite to leave an extra 10 to 15 per cent in expensive restaurants and some loose change in tavernas and little restaurants. Porters and guides should be given a reasonable tip, and anywhere else that you receive extra special service. Be careful not to offend local Greeks who offer help or advice by tipping them; they are just being friendly.

Toilets
Greek toilets are traditionally a bit primitive, and not always pleasant to use. Often a bin is

provided for paper as this can block the small-bore plumbing system. As there are few public toilets, order a coffee or a drink, and use the toilet in a taverna or café. Those in hotels are far better, and improving all the time.

Tourist Information Offices

There are local tourist offices or tourist police on most of the islands in the main towns and tourist resorts. They can usually be found in the town hall, and offer information on accommodation and transport. In the Athens branches of the Greek National Tourist Office (GNTO/EOT) you can get plenty of information on all of the regions in Greece and schedules for the inter-island ferries which should be used only as guidelines. Other details of ferries, buses and trains can also be collected here. Request information in advance from the National Tourist Organization of Greece at:

UK
4 Conduit Street,
London W1R 0DJ
☎ 0171 734 5997.

USA
645 Fifth Avenue, Olympic Tower, New York. 10022
☎ (212) 421-5777.

Canada
1233 rue de la Montaigne,
Montreal, Quebec H3G 1Z2
☎ (514) 871 1535.

Australia
51-57 Pitt Street, Sydney,
NSW 2000

☎ 2411 663/4.

Tours see **Excursions**

Transport

If you are hopping from island to island, the main means of transport will be a ferry. Some

people pick one island which offers quite a few different ferries, and use that main

A horse-drawn carriage in Aegina Town – one of the more leisurely ways to get around.

island as their base while they explore the surrounding places. Others like to travel as far as they can and see as much as possible in the time at their disposal. Either way you need to be patient, as ferries can easily be cancelled in poor weather – very high winds, for example – and services can be erratic.

Tickets may be bought from local agents, or on the boat. The most reliable information on schedules and sailings comes from the port police who can be found on all islands. The word 'ferries' covers everything from the fast and expensive hydrofoils and the medium-sized to large ferry boats which operate the main services, to small ferries and caique.

Bus services vary from island to island, and timetables are usually posted beside main stops. In the busiest season there is usually an undignified scrummage for the bus, as queues do not exist and everyone fights for a place.

Taxis are a good way to see an island, particularly if you can share the cost with a group of people; negotiate the price in advance. Taxis are usually waiting to take late-night revellers from the main tourist spots to their hotels or rooms,

and are not expensive. *See also* **Tourist Information Offices.**

TV and Radio

Privately owned television stations outnumber Government-controlled stations, but the latter broadcast English news summaries in the early evenings. Many foreign stations can be received all over Greece with the appropriate aerial, satellite dish or cable hook-up. The Greek Radio Station broadcasts a news bulletin at 0730 on ERT/EPT 1, and the many local Greek radio stations also have English-language news programmes and bulletins, and tourist information.

Vaccinations see Before You Go p.108

Water (drinking, shortage, etc.)

Water can be a scarce commodity in some areas, particularly in the Cyclades in the height of summer, therefore try not to waste any. Sometimes the supply is turned off during the day. The water is safe to drink and usually tastes very good, but bottled water is available everywhere if you are not sure.

Youth Hostels see Accommodation

INDEX